THE TAROT

Published and distributed in the U.S.
by Stewart, Tabori and Chang,
a division of U.S. Media Holdings, INC.
575 Broadway, New York, N.Y. 10012

Distributed in Canada by
General Publishing Co. Ltd.
30 Lesmill Road, Don Mills, Ontario
Canada, M3B 2T6

ISBN 1-55670-504-2

Project Editor: *Liz Wheeler*
Editor: *Lol Henderson*
Art Editor: *Vicky Harvey*
Picture Research: *Sharon Hutton*
Production: *Garry Lewis*

Printed and bound in Italy

THE TAROT

THE TRADITIONAL TAROT REINTERPRETED FOR THE MODERN WORLD

ADAM FRONTERAS

STEWART
TABORI
& CHANG

Contents

FOREWORD *6-7*

THE HISTORY AND MYSTERY OF THE TAROT *8*

Early Playing Cards and the First Tarot Decks *8*

The Design of Early Cards *10*

Contentious Cards *12*

From Gambling to Divining *13*

THE OCCULT DEVELOPMENT OF THE TAROT *14*

Freemasons, the Occult, and the Golden Dawn *16*

THE ARCHETYPAL TAROT *19*

Seeing Beyond the Obvious *20*

PSYCHIC ABILITIES *21*

CHOOSING AND RELATING TO A DECK *22*

Giving Your Cards Meaning *23*

Placing the Cards   26

THE MAJOR ARCANA   27

THE MINOR ARCANA   28
Astrology and the Minor Arcana Suits   28

THE MAJOR ARCANA CARD BY CARD   30

THE MINOR ARCANA CARD BY CARD   74

PLACING AND READING THE CARDS   104

THE ASTROLOGICAL CIRCLE   104

THE CELTIC CROSS SPREAD   111

THE TRANSFORMATION   114

THE THREE-CARD SPREAD   122

THE NAME SPREAD   124

Further Reading   128
Acknowledgements   128

FOREWORD

Your first reaction to this book may be just to regard it as yet another book on Tarot. However, if you read on a little you will find that it is refreshingly different.

There are many general books on the subject, but Adam has intentionally written about the original ideas and interpretations, meaning that this book will be of real benefit to those wanting to use any Tarot deck proficiently, regardless of the story or mythical themes in a particular deck. This book will become a classic for those learning the Tarot and an important addition to the shelves of those who are already accomplished in the art of divining.

Adam has been involved in the esoteric fields for many years, not only in the art of Tarot but, also a proficient tutor and interpreter in the disciplines of Astrology and I Ching.

The British Astrological & Psychic Society deems it an honour to list within its Register of

Approved Consultant-Members the name of Adam Fronteras, who traveled around Britain in his teenage years giving readings at exhibitions with the Society's Founder, Russell Grant, and is thus remembered by the public when he attends the Festival of Mind, Body & Spirit in London, England, on the Society's stand.

It has long been the aim of the British Astrological & Psychic society to increase its teaching role, as specified by the Society's Founder, in the many fields covered by the Consultant-Members of BAPS. Therefore, this book will become the mainstay of the Foundation Course of the British Astrological & Psychic Society's Tarot School.

Berenice Watt
President of The British Astrological & Psychic Society
[Author – *The Language of the Psycards*, Alexander Press]

September 1995

THE HISTORY AND
MYSTERY OF THE TAROT

Fear is a common reaction to Tarot cards. Why is that? Where do the cards come from and where does the history and mystery of the Tarot begin? The history of the Tarot shares the history of playing cards. To read the Tarot as a consultant you do not need to know the history, but should you be interested in learning about it and then passing on your knowledge, it is important that you know the true history, rather than the misleading versions perpetuated by critics. Unfortunately, many books have added to the fear and misunderstanding; one really has to peel away the myths and look at the facts. The lack of an accurate history makes those that use the Tarot prey to critics and historians that link the emergence of Tarot cards to occultists, implying that because the occultist view of history is false, then the Tarot is false. However, the Tarot works not because it is an ancient Egyptian set of cards but because the images are archetypal and deeply embedded within the images of life around us.

Early Playing Cards and the First Tarot Decks

The earliest Tarot decks that survive today are the Visconti-Sforza decks. Since these fifteenth-century decks there have been many variations. In the last thirty years, there have been hundreds of deck designs, from such artists as Salvador Dali and Furgas Hall, who designed the deck Jane Seymour read from in the James Bond film *Live And Let Die*. The most famous early deck, the Visconti-Sforza, contain figures and faces of what are thought to be close family members.

The earliest playing cards came from ninth-century China, about the same time as the first books were printed. However, apart from a Money suit there is very little direct similarity between Chinese and European decks. There is no evidence of intermediate development between the Chinese and European decks, so it is unlikely that one grew out of the other, but we cannot rule out the possibility altogether.

Some have argued that Muslims developed the Tarot cards, but the oldest decks existing from the Muslim world are more recent than references to European decks, so any transfer is likely to have been from Europe to the Arab world.

Another possibility is India, where most cards were circular and usually

Roger Moore and Jane Seymour in Live And Let Die

consisted of eight suits of twelve cards. Although there are no references to these before the sixteenth century, there is an obvious link to European cards in general.

The earliest playing card decks in Europe date from 1377. Through the next five hundred years references to them deal with their use in gambling and the bans issued against them. The fact that fortunetelling is not mentioned would imply that it is a more modern usage.

The Design Of Early Cards

In 1377 in Basle, Switzerland, a Dominican friar, John, described playing cards. There were four suits; each suit consisted of thirteen cards (ten plus three court cards). These would have been single-headed cards; doubleheaded cards as a pattern came about in 1850. The suits of cards are still with us today and little has changed. European decks sometimes keep their original suit names of Cups, Swords, Batons, and Coins, which later became Hearts, Spades, Clubs, and Diamonds. The Tarot in general has kept to the original European names, though more recently replacing Batons with Wands, and Coins with Pentacles. There are some variations, such as the German standard of Leaves, Acorns, Hearts, and Bells.

The earliest cards were copied by hand, consequently, designs incorporate the social and religious themes of the day. The Devil card in the Tarot, for example, has horns and cloven feet. Prior to Christianity, the pagan culture worshipped the god of nature, known as Pan or Cernunnow, who was represented as a horned god. Gradually, the Christian church called the old god evil. The gods of the old religion became the devils of the new religion. In the church of Notre Dame in Paris, recent archeological

Above: Pan, the god of nature, here drawn by Maxfield Parrish

Right: Cathedral of Notre Dame on the Ile de la Cité in Paris, France

excavations have revealed a stone altar with a statue of Cernunnos; Notre Dame was built on the site of an ancient pagan place of worship. The Devil card, therefore, stands both as a record of changing religious beliefs and, in its iconic context, as a symbol of passive acceptance of fate.

From the fifteenth to the eighteenth century the principle method of printing was with engraved woodcuts. However, the very wealthy could afford to employ an artist to handpaint a deck, even featuring their own likeness on, for instance, the King of Cups. By the late-sixteenth century, cards were being produced by wood block printing in significant numbers, with the size of the deck varying from fifty to ninety-seven cards from town to town. The output from Marseilles, France, was greater than that of other towns, making the design from there the most widely known. The Marseilles Tarot became the model layout and description for most Tarot cards.

Contentious Cards

The production and use of playing cards became an important moral and political issue. In 1397 the Prévôt de Paris forbade "working people from playing tennis, ball, cards, or ninepins exempting only on holidays." In Venice, in 1441, a ban on imported cards was enforced by the authorities after lobbying from local printers.

In the continuing debate over the exact origins of playing cards and Tarot decks, it has been suggested that it is possible the standard deck of playing cards was brought into India from China, then from India through the Arab countries into Europe (Spain or Italy) by travelling gypsies. The Romany language of the gypsies is very close to Sanskrit, the holy tongue of the Hindus and is one of the oldest known languages. However, the Tarot is a European invention, occurring some sixty years later than standard playing cards appeared. The oldest cards still in existence, often cited as the original set of Tarot decks, date from 1392. These were supposedly specially painted by Jacquemin Gringoneur for King Charles VI of

France. However, the cards King Charles paid for were never described in detail at the time, and, just to confuse matters even more, the ones in the Bibliothèque Nationale in France ascribed to him are dated some hundred years later.

From Gambling to Divining

The word Tarot was first used in 1442 in the Court of Trionfi, which was the Italian word for Tarot. From this root word we get the word trumps – some refer to the Major Arcana as trump cards. The modern game of trumps, or whist, originates from the game of trionfi, played with what is now known as the Tarot deck.

In 1457 the Tarot as an expanded deck for gambling purposes was mentioned in Florence. The first court cards consisted of King, Cavalier (Knight), and Jack (Page). Italian decks added the Queen in the 1500s.

In 1488 Galcottus Martius began to explore possible uses other than gaming. At around the same time Count Matteo Maria Boirdo wrote a small opera of sonnets around each of the major cards.

In Venice in 1540, Francesco Marcolini da Forli published a work that used playing cards for fortunetelling, though more as an oracle than as a means of predicting the future. It was in the 1780s that the Tarot was first used for fortunetelling proper. With the advent of the occult revival in the late 1700s, came the development of the Tarot as a divination aid rather than just as a means of attempting to predict the future.

It has also been suggested that this use of cards is based on a book published in 1526 by Fanti of Ferrara, in which he linked the numerical values of the cards to four line stanzas, using a circular dial with 21 figures. 21 numbers are easy to adjust to the 22 figures of the Major Arcana and their associated meanings. The numbers were chosen by spinning a pointer or a central plate, similar to playing a roulette wheel.

The Occult Development of the Tarot

The connection of the occult tradition to the Tarot is well established. The first exponent of the Tarot and its influence was Antoine Court de Gebelin (1719-1784). Court de Gebelin was a mason who wrote a nine-volume work entitled *Le Monde Primitif* (The Primitive World). This primitive world was based on an idea that perpetuates in many occult circles of a golden age of man, when all people shared a common language and culture.

In his eighth volume, published in 1781, he turns to the Tarot pack. From this small beginning, the whole occult history of the Tarot has mushroomed. Court de Gebelin describes how he was playing the game of Tarot when he had an inspiration that the Tarot derived from ancient Egyptian religion. To quote Michael Dummett, "At the time, of course, Egyptian hieroglyphics had not yet been deciphered by Champollion but, to a man of de Gebelin's intuitive gifts, that was no great obstacle, and he was able to inform us that the word Tarot meant the Royal Road, being derived from the ancient Egyptian 'tar' meaning way and 'row' meaning royal." Neither word is in Wallis Budge's Egyptian dictionary.

Etteilla, a professional clairvoyant and astrologer in Paris in the late 1700s, wrote a number of books and was the first known writer of reversed meanings for cards. He claimed that the Tarot originated in Egypt, and that it was devised by a committee of magicians one hundred and seventy-one years before the great flood of the Old Testament. The first Tarot cards, according to Etteilla, were inscribed on leaves of gold.

Around this time there were arguments as to what order the Tarot should be arranged in, particularly the major cards. This was a result of people moving the cards around to fit their individual theories. Etteilla formed a Tarot "college" that produced a number of profes-

Eliphas Levi, publisher of many books on magic in the nineteenth century

sional Tarot consultants. Unfortunately, he did not relish competition from his students; in a later work, he praises a couple of his pupils and denounces the other 150 as charlatans – not very noble after presumably charging them for the education he gave them. Etteilla also produced the first revised set of Tarot cards based on his interpretations.

A prodigy of Etteilla's, Marie-Anne Adelaide Lenormande, was clairvoyant to Empress Josephine in the early 1800s and from her

deck a number of variations of Tarot cards started to be printed.

Eliphas Levi (born Alphonse-Louis Constant) changed his name in 1852 after developing a fascination for magic. He published books on ritual magic that are still highly regarded today. In his books he links the Tarot with the Jewish Cabbala, and the twenty-two letters of the Hebrew alphabet to the twenty-two Major Arcana. Levi said of the Tarot, "An imprisoned person with no other book than the Tarot, if he knew how to use it, could in a few years acquire universal knowledge, and would be able to speak on all subjects with unequaled learning and inexhaustible eloquence."

In 1887, Oswald Wirth, an amateur artist, met Levi and was inspired to repaint the Tarot with an Egyptian theme. This was the first version of the Tarot to be associated solely with the occult.

Freemasons, the Occult, and the Golden Dawn

At around this time, the Freemasons' influence began to grow. Its occult branches, such as the Grand Order of the

Above and left: Justice and the Emperor from the Papus Tarot deck

Rose Cross, used the Tarot, propagating further definitions.

A major development of occult Tarot was propagated by Dr Gerald Encausse, a doctor who published a few medical works but a vast amount on all aspects of occultism, until he died in World War I. In 1889, writing under the pseudonym Dr. Papus, he states in *The Tarot of the Bohemians*, "The book of Thoth (the Tarot) it is the book of Adam, it is the book of the primitive revaluation of ancient civilizations." Also, the terms Major and Minor Arcana are first used here. Papus also talks about the strong numerological links with the Tarot.

The introduction of the Tarot in British history is largely through the Hermetic Order of the Golden Dawn; among its members were a number of illustrious people, including W. B. Yeats. Dr. William Wynn Westcott, one of the founders of the Golden Dawn, took a strong interest in the Tarot and it played a large part in Golden Dawn teachings.

In 1910 Arthur Edward Waite wrote *The Key to the Tarot* and had a new style of deck painted by Pamela Coleman Smith. This has become the standard Tarot deck employed most often today.

As these various authors proposed their theories to explain the origins, numerical sequences, and individual meanings, others acted upon them,

9 THE HERMIT

Top: W B Yeats
Above: An example of a card from the Golden Dawn deck

Above: Aleister Crowley, publisher of the Book of Thoth *in 1944*

including Aleister Crowley (once described by the *Daily Express* as the wickedest man in the world). Crowley joined the Golden Dawn in 1900 but was later banned. In 1944 he self-published the *Book of Thoth*, with a deck by Lady Frieda Harris, who was a disciple of Crowley. At the time she was also wife of a leading Liberal politician. During this time other decks appeared from Golden Dawn offshoots in America, such as decks from Paul Foster Case and Dr. Francis Israel Regardie.

Above: Examples from the Aleister Crowley Thoth Tarot deck, designed by Lady Frieda Harris

THE ARCHETYPAL TAROT

The images of the Tarot are founded on archetypal symbols that can be seen in many cultures. These basic symbols form links between different cultures and are of fundamental importance to humankind's mystic beliefs. For example, The Fool can be recognized as the pagan fool of the Mummer Plays, Morris Dancing, the Sannyasin of Buddhist beliefs, and Dionysus (or Bacchus) of Greek culture.

The collective wisdom of the Tarot has its derivatives in the pagan and Gnostic religions that had their center in Alexandria in the second century A.D. and flourished well into the fourth century. Gnosticism mixed together Indian, Chaldean, Persian, and Egyptian magical doctrines and seasoned them with Greek philosophy and Hebrew cabalistic beliefs. Gnostic wisdom was, in turn, handed down through the centuries, inherited by unorthodox sects who, with the rise in power of the Christian church by the Middle Ages, were ruthlessly persecuted and forced underground or stamped out.

It was, oddly enough, the Christian church that unwittingly preserved many of the pagan doctrines and lores preached by heretical Christian sects such as the Knights Templar. Although the sects themselves were systematically crushed within the walls of the Christian monasteries, the monks thought it wise to learn about and document the heretical beliefs that threatened the sanctity of their church, to arm themselves with the knowledge to recognize any insurgencies – so much so that the Vatican contains some of the best astrological works, even a bath painted with the signs of the zodiac.

In this way, pagan knowledge was preserved intact and relatively secret in monastic manuscripts. It was through the secret studies of the Freemasons and Rosicrucian lodges that an interest in the Tarot and related occult sciences, such as astrology and alchemy, were kept alive.

The tremendous world changes that occurred in the late nineteenth and early twentieth centuries, especially the advent of two world wars, prevented a complete popularization of occult sciences; only as a result of the comparative stability and wealth of the last two decades has specialist literature become readily available.

The shock of the world wars and a general disenchantment with our science-led consumer society has created a need for a spiritual satisfaction in life.

Seeing Beyond the Obvious

Looking more closely at archetypes in the Tarot cards themselves, it is useful to examine why the most feared card in the pack is Death. It must be emphasized that this card does not literally mean physical death but change, or regeneration. The symbol is of a skeleton with a scythe, representing a sweeping away of the past to make a fresh start. Thus, fear of this card is unfounded, as are most of the commonly preconceived worries about the Tarot's archetypes.

Some say the shuffling of a pack of cards can have no reflection on your future. This is true, but misses the point; it is important to remember that the cards themselves do not hold any magic, they just provide visual guidance to the readers, who must then use their psychic powers for interpretation. The cards are only an aid to give the telepathic and clairvoyant talents of the reader a push in the right direction. In fact, in all of the intuitive sciences, whether Tarot, crystal ball, tea leaf, or even beer glass readings, the physical items act merely as aids to concentration and are not ends in themselves.

I MOON

Above: The Merlin deck by Robert Stewart

PSYCHIC ABILITIES

The term "psychic" usually refers to the ability to perceive or sense things beyond the normal range of the five physical senses. This is often called a sixth sense. There is a psychic, or subtle perception sense, corresponding to each of the physical senses. Everyone is potentially psychic, and just as some people have one or more aspect of their physical being and physical perception more highly developed than another, some people have a natural ability to function on psychic levels. The fact that many people who had never considered themselves to be psychic have, with proper training, developed this kind of perception, shows that this potential exists in everyone.

Above: The Prediction deck by Bernard Stringer

Of course, those with natural psychic ability will, with training and practice, generally be capable of more advanced forms of psychic work than others. This, of course, is no different to a comparison between those who have a natural musical or artistic ability and those who do not.

Being psychic is, therefore, not something unusual or to be feared, for everyone possesses the ability to a degree, even if they do not recognize it. The techniques and methodologies of psychism can be taught and, with practice, will form the foundation of a person's particular talent. This cannot be measured and defined in a linear or scientific manner anymore than the aesthetics of playing a musical instrument or the painting of a picture can be measured exactly.

Each person will tend to develop his or her own style of using their psychic ability. In all cases though, it is still results that count, especially for someone working as a professional in any of the predictive arts.

Choosing and Relating to a Deck

Selecting a suitable deck of Tarot cards can be a problem. The beginner is confronted by a bewildering array of designs, differing in size, color, historical and symbolic content, and price! The deck featured in this book is a classic design, and although certain details may influence your readings, the most important factor is the emotional and intuitive link that grows between you and your cards.

According to tradition, cards should be given not bought. This stems from the age-old notion that spirit and matter do not mix, that "money is the root of all evil," tainting whatever it touches. Such idealism is less fashionable today, but many people still find they form a stronger bond with a pack that has the positive association of being presented to them by a loved one, rather than one obtained through a cold commercial transaction. However, you may not feel in tune with the designs someone else has selected.

The ideal way to relate to a pack is to make them your own through learning the individual cards. Try to think of friends (or foes) who epitomize the essence of each card as you learn it; form firm associations so that whenever you see the card the individual comes to mind. This creative act is extremely important for two reasons: first, the imaginative energy is in itself magical and tends to generate power. There is a sense in which each time you think of something you are personally bringing it into existence. Second, creativity focuses your thoughts as you make decisions about the content and meaning of a card. Think about how you would make a collage on the theme of either the Fool or the World. The process of searching for suitable images, selecting some and rejecting others, and being conscious of your reasons for these choices is an essential aid to memory and learning. You should also consider that the end result says something about your character. Compare your efforts with those of a friend to see where different emphases lie.

Giving Your Cards Meaning

Sympathy towards your cards is crucial. You are going to be pouring your energy into them, investing them with power, and treating them with a certain reverence so it is essential that you do not find them ugly, garish, or alien to you. No cards are intrinsically powerful; success depends upon the meaning that you give them.

It is a good idea to make some sort of symbolic act of identification with your first set of cards. Some people go as far as consecrating their cards, using the four elements to free them of past associations and dedicate them to their new role. This is unnecessary, but a welcoming gesture, such as removing the packaging and rewrapping the cards in silk while thinking positively, helps to establish the correct attitude. This sort of minor ritual can be performed at any time – so if you already have a pack you can "renew" them in this way. It can be particularly beneficial after giving a reading to someone you dislike, as your feelings about them could linger and affect later spreads.

Such acts are not intended to be "occult." Ritual is best described as a functional support to faith and concentration; it should act as a key to lead you into the desired state of mind before you commence a reading. To use it most successfully you must make a habit of establishing a calm and receptive attitude each time you get the Tarot out. Work out a sequence of ritual you intend to perform, perhaps just several deep breaths and several mental or spoken repetitions. Alternatively, burn incense, throw salt into the air, offer prayers to the deity of your choice, or bow to the four points of the compass. Whatever you do should not be too complicated or ridiculous. The intention is to draw your thoughts together and expel tension, not to make yourself feel silly, which has the reverse effect. Once you have rehearsed these thoughts or actions about thirty times before laying the cards you will find that the sensation of peace and openness that you aim for comes readily when the ritual is begun.

Preserve Their Uniqueness

Since you intend to use your cards for divination they should be treated as sacred objects and kept away from mundane influences. Again, this is not to suggest that the cards themselves are special, rather that you will find your ability to read them accurately enhanced if you respect and believe in them.

Any power that they have is bestowed upon them by you, and it is not easy to pour your psychic energies into things that are left lying around collecting dust. Traditionally, sacred objects are kept out of contact with the profane as their power drains out of them, and mankind loses its source of mediation with the divine. (Think of the red carpets laid for royalty; the monarch's sacred heel is not meant to touch the earth.) Consequently, it is wise to wrap the cards in silk and – if possible – keep them in a wooden box.

Silk wrapping used for storage can be of any color, however, you should also try to use a silk cloth to lay the cards on when giving readings, and in this case you may want to vary the color based on the nature of the question.

Generally, the following applications are suitable:

Love/relationships	–	Green or pink
Money	–	Yellow or gold
Intellect/education	–	Gray
Career/status	–	Purple
Character	–	Blue
Health	–	Brown/green

At this point you may be wondering how many cloths, boxes, and other bits of paraphernalia you are going to need and whether it is really worth the effort. This depends upon how seriously you propose to take your studies. Trappings, like ritual, serve as aids to concentration, and as with many other things, you will find that the more trouble you take with the Tarot, the more rewarding it will prove. Certainly clients are unconsciously influenced by the presentation of a reading. Cards that emerge swathed in silk from a curiously wrought wooden box and are then laid upon flamboyant cloths make a more dramatic and convincing impression than those that are taken from a torn and tattered cardboard sheath and strewn across the kitchen table. These "tools of the trade" help to make a reading an experience that goes beyond the familiar and mundane. They also give the novice an authority and credibility behind which true confidence can develop. In many ways these touches are more important to the beginner than the experienced consultant.

Reversed Meanings

Reversed meanings are a modern invention; many of the early decks had pictures only for the Major Arcana and simple pip cards (marked like dice) for the suits. Many decks show the Minor Arcana with doubleheaded court cards, the same as a modern deck of standard cards. It is, therefore, impossible, without marking the cards, to come up with reversed meanings. However, though the notion of a reversed meaning does not share the same history as the cards, it is no less valid. Just as harmonics and asteroids have added to the interpretative skills of the astrologer, so reversed readings add to the divination of a skilled reader. This said, their use in modern Tarot readings is still something of an enigma. Many books ignore the influences of reversed cards, and some modern decks make reversed reading impossible, such as the circular Mother Piece deck.

You can tell the reversed cards easily in a deck that has pictures all the way through. When laying out the cards it is always a good idea to lay all the cards of the spread out; if many more cards are reversed than the right way up, the pack has been handed back to you reversed. Reading reversed cards is similar to retrograde planets in astrology. They do not mean the opposite, rather they hint at greater delays and obstacles associated with the meaning of the card the right way around. They can have a delayed, or hidden meaning, sometimes good, sometimes bad. For instance, the Knight of Pentacles usually indicates someone putting projects into action and a new career opportunity. In a reversed position this card indicates obstacles and delays, but, it also shows that these are under one's own control; the person must simply try harder to put the plans into action.

Reversed meanings must never be dogmatic, and you may feel at the time that giving the standard interpretation is more correct.

When recollecting the cards from the reading do not go through the deck turning the cards the right way round. Tarot is about synchronicity; if cards were turned the wrong way around in a reading but not used, it is probable that they are there for a reason, possibly your for next client. In conclusion, a reversed card is a modifier.

Placing the Cards

Most Tarot readers place the cards in predetermined patterns known as spreads or layouts (see pages 104-127 for a selection of spread configurations and readings).

Some readers prefer to simply lay out one card at a time and interpret them as they are, but laying in spreads provides a method for concentrating on individual areas of life. If there were no distinct formulas or sequences in mathematics, numbers would be meaningless. Similarly with the Tarot, if we just deal out the cards singly, we have no idea which area of life each card represents. A coherent structure also helps to guide the seeker in understanding the reading and keeps the information in chronological order. Spreads have evolved as useful structures for clearly presenting information on all areas of a subject's life.

Place the cards so that you can see each one clearly; if a card is partially obscured you may miss an important element. This is particularly true for beginners who are not completely familiar with their cards. Do not begin to interpret immediately, pause for a few moments to allow your feelings for the cards to rise from your unconscious and crystallize in your conscious thoughts.

THE MAJOR ARCANA

The Major Arcana are the most influential cards in the Tarot deck. Indeed, a few readers use only the Major Arcana cards. The Major Arcana are made up of virtues, such as Temperance; astrological bodies, such as the Sun and Moon; and religious characters, such as the High Priest and the Emperor, which rule the kings and queens of the Minor Arcana.

On life's journey, the Major Arcana represent the cities that people pass through and the Minor Arcana the villages and towns; the major and minor influences on life. The Major Arcana often represent significant turning points in life with effect at a deep, personal level, while the Minor Arcana represent more transient experiences.

Although the pictorial symbolism in each card has certain general meanings, the full significance and relevance of each card can only be gained if the reader understands the deeper meanings of the symbols. The next chapter will try to explain some of these meanings. For example, red and white are used throughout the Tarot for the coloring of clothes and images. This color usage stems from early pagan fertility rites, where white represented semen, and red, the menstrual blood. Today, the maypole's red and white coloring is a reminder of pagan beliefs. You must always pay careful attention to all the details in any particular card, as it is not just the main character or symbol that will reveal its mystical significance in the Tarot. Each card is also identified by a Roman numeral. In the next chapter this number is used for an interpretation of the card's numerological significance. Each character is introduced with a look at its historical roots, the basis for our understanding of it in the Tarot. It is important to remember that different positions in the spread can affect the meaning of a card.

The astrological influences given are those that the author has found useful when marrying the two arts. There is no fixed astrological correspondence; there are many different ideas concerning which planet rules which card.

THE MINOR ARCANA

More than two-thirds of the Tarot is made up of suited cards similar to those found in ordinary playing packs. In fact, the Minor Arcana derive from our familiar fifty-two card decks, which were widely used before the invention and addition of the twenty-two trumps to form the Tarot. Hearts, diamonds, clubs, and spades stem from the Spanish names for the four suits and are equivalent to the Tarot's cups, pentacles, wands, and swords. These cards describe the bulk of our lives, the day-to-day events and opportunities, leaving the twenty-two major trumps to show the rarer intervention of fate.

Astrology and the Minor Arcana Suits
The Swords (or Spades)

Linked with the Fire signs (Aries, Leo and Sagittarius), often these cards are wrongly attributed to Air. The sword in magic represents Fire and is used as a test of strength and courage at the commencement of initiation, particularly in western magic practices. It is interesting that to the occult, the story of young Arthur and the sword in the stone, has a deeper meaning than is commonly realized. Finding the sword was a test of strength and represents his initiation, from whence he became aware of his royal heritage and the quest he would face as King Arthur. The set of Swords represents strength, action, and challenge, and are related more closely to the Fire signs than the Air signs that some books suggest. Swords are created in fire (the geological process as well as the forge) for use in asserting the strength, leadership, and willpower that typify Aries, Leo and Sagittarius.

The Wands

In many packs these may be called batons, rods, or clubs. They are linked to Air (Gemini, Libra, and Aquarius). The Wands, like the trees from which they are made, are affected by the air but are adaptable and independent. Because the trees represent knowledge (the Tree of Knowledge in the Garden of Eden and the Druids' alphabet, based on the names of trees), they are more powerful than force. The Wands also signify travel, among other things.

The Pentacles

Sometimes called coins or diamonds. The Pentacles, linked to earth, represent the most practical sides of life, such as work, finances, and buying and selling. They can, therefore, be easily linked in with the signs of Capricorn, Taurus, and Virgo.

The Cups

Linked with the Heart and the emotional Water signs of Cancer, Scorpio, and Pisces.

The Elements

The idea of four elements has been part of occult and psychological theory from the Greeks through Jung, and it fits the four suits rather aptly. Cups and Coins are generally taken to represent water and earth, but the attributions of Swords and Staves are often disputed. To fit their magical practices, the Golden Dawn linked staves with fire, and swords with the remaining element – air. However, other authorities associate swords with fire and action, and staves with air and intellect. Symbolically, the second view is more appropriate – swords are forged in fire and intended for use in battle. In astrology swords belong to Mars, the hot, dry planet ruling fevers and wounds, iron and steel, and the warrior god. However, a staff is made from strong but supple wood. Trees draw nourishment from air but are destroyed by fire. A staff is used to support and protect travelers – on mental and physical journeys – and is traditionally a symbol of Mercury.

THE MAJOR ARCANA –
CARD BY CARD

0
THE FOOL

The Fool is Alpha and Omega, both the beginning and end of the major cards. Thus, he is numberless, zero and twenty-two. He is pure spirit and air, searching for a direction, a new life. He is the acolyte looking for initiation into life's mysteries, but, when he finds it, he is still a fool. His quest is naively pure; to be pure is to be wise, so the Fool is also wise.

He derives from the horned god Bacchus (or the Roman Dionysius), the incarnate power of spiritual revolt and rebirth and the god of wine. Bacchanals were revered by pagans, who believed that when drunk they experienced mystical enlightenment. His image altered subtly; donkey's ears or feathers replaced the horns; gradually, the court fool, or jester, emerged with the familiar cap, bells, and pig's bladder. Exempt from royal retribution, the court fool's jokes were often outrageous.

He is a carefree Geminian personality,

skipping ahead with his few belongings and his little dog at his side. With his staff, he carries a white rose, a symbol of purity reflected in the red and white of his garments. The feather and laurel wreath represent connection with pagan gods of nature. The bleak brown rocks represent the solid support of a past that wasn't always happy, the blue mountains the future and its rewards, with the sun lighting the way. The dog jumps at him representing his conscience as well as people, such as his parents, who try to hold him back for their own security. His fickle Geminian personality can and will leave these people and past events behind.

Meaning

The Fool represents someone throwing off people and restrictions from the past, and setting off in search of new pastures. In contrast, it can also reflect the attitudes of others toward the subject, their belief that his decisions and actions are foolish. They will try to hold him back.

This card generally indicates that someone needs to start again, taking no decision lightly, avoiding the disaster that impulsiveness could cause. If all choices and likely outcomes are honestly considered, the result will be positive.

Reversed Meaning

When reversed, the card shows that the subject has no real direction and should refrain from taking impulsive decisions as they would be regretted. Or, the subject feels that a close friend is making a wrong decision, the result of an erratic, impulsive nature, and wants to steer him or her back to the right path.

Astrological Influence

Uranus

I
THE MAGICIAN

The Magician is a juggler or conjurer in medieval designs, but the qualities of a magician are closer to the card's true significance.

The Magician in the Tarot comes from the god Hermes. He is cunning, fast, skilful, a flatterer, and, as his Italian name, Bagatto, indicates, a gossip.

The Magician is another Geminian card. Mercury, Gemini's ruler, endows the character with skillful adaptability. Like the Fool, he wears red and white robes and a belt. However, the Magician's green belt signifies the highest degree of skill and knowledge in magic practices. The belt is a serpent, representing life, death, and rebirth.

On the Magician's altar are four objects, representing the elements and the suits of the Tarot's Minor Arcana. On either side of the Magician are flowers, white representing male and red representing female. He points up with his magic wand, showing spiritual mastery. His left hand points down to the earth, making the sign of the horned god with his fingers, indicating control of the material plane and self-protection.

This means he will guide us on the higher, spiritual path. Behind the Magician stands the castle wall, representing the wall of energy, or the magic circle. Above him is the sign of infinity, signifying all life is endless and individual power is boundless. The Magician's number is one, representing the beginning, independence, being alone and self-possessed.

Meaning

The card represents someone skillful, cunning, and adaptable, willing to teach and learn. Powerful, intelligent, and an open-minded teacher, thoughtful and understanding of other people and how to help them.

The Magician does not try to judge or restrain others; he knows that people must be allowed to learn from mistakes.

The Magician is the card of the doctor, the psychologist. It can indicate a new voyage of learning, a new skill, or even a fresh career, but caution must be taken; plan carefully when making such important decisions over the coming few months.

Reversed Meaning

When reversed it can show the materialist side of the skillful man, the con-man, and trickster, perhaps the unscrupulous salesman. It shows the deceitful greedy person who, through skill and eloquence, can harm others. The seeker should not make any decision that is materially based, as any resulting success may be short-lived.

Downfall may follow due to the seeker's obstinacy and inability to adapt to changes; an entirely different approach needs to be taken.

Astrological Influence

Mercury

II
THE HIGH PRIESTESS

THE HIGH PRIESTESS

In some decks, the High Priestess is known as the female Pope or Juno, deriving from pagan religions that had an earth goddess.

The High Priestess represents the moon goddess, wearing a moon crown and with a symbol of the moon at her feet. She is known as the queen of Heaven, or as Isis the goddess of fertility. However, she symbolizes duality; creativity and destruction, light and dark, and in the latter aspect she is known as Persephone, queen of the underworld, or as the queen of death. The Christian Mary took over the role, known as Stella Maris (Star of the Sea), or Venus, the planet that protects sailors, because by rising and setting before the sun it is a useful aid in navigation. Strangely, Venus is also associated with Lucifer.

The astrological influences are obvious as she represents the moon goddess. As silver is the metal of the moon, she wears a silver cross. Pisces is represented, showing spirituality, understanding, and a need to help others.

Her number is two, represented by the

Hebrew letter Gimel, meaning knowledge and power. She sits between a black and a white pillar – the two aspects of magic. Many magic temples have two pillars, representing positive (white) and negative (black) influences.

The veil of pomegranates behind her hides the psychic side of life, represented by the water in the background. The blue and purple colors indicate the Piscean aspect of the card. She holds the scroll of the Jewish law (the Torah), which also holds the secrets of life and the universe.

Meaning

When this card appears it shows a person of knowledge and learning, someone who is willing to help. It can show a very psychic person or someone who uses his or her mind effectively. This card also has a practical side; with the water and moon, it can show the menstrual cycle and when reversed can show problems in this area. Thought is needed; the seeker should seek help and guidance from someone he or she respects. The seeker also needs to use intuition as this will give considerable direction in how to proceed. The card suggests success in developing talents, especially those connected with the psychic arts. It shows someone with inner wisdom.

Reversed Meaning

A card of many facets, asking more questions than it answers. It can show deep psychological problems, difficulty with conception or with relating to other people. The card can indicate illness for the seeker; they should beware of emotional stress. Someone who has risen to a high position but will fail if too vain and selfish.

Astrological Influence

Moon

III
THE EMPRESS

The number of the Empress is three, which numerologically signifies creation, the essence of this card. The Empress represents the pagan goddess mother earth and also the Greek goddess Demeter. She is mother nature or Gaia, the earth goddess. In the Norse religions, she is Freyja, remembered now by the day Friday.

As earth mother and as Demeter, she is patron of nature; growth, fertility, protector of the harvest, and all matters of health and nourishment. Harvest festivals date from the pagan earth goddess festivals.

Boadicea, Cleopatra, and Theodora of the Byzantines all regarded themselves as the mothers of their respective empires, and have influenced the Empress archetype. Theodora's appearance on some Empress cards strongly suggests Christian influence in the card's development.

In astrology she is Cancer, a water sign representing home and family. Again, the natural ruler of the sign is the moon, but more of the mother aspect.

The surrounding land is fertile and brimming with trees and plants, representing the fertility of the landscape and of nature. The green clothes of the figure emphasize this, and the Empress appears to be pregnant. A lake, representing the element water, is fed by a waterfall, indicating the subconscious and the natural psychic connection that mothers have with their offspring. The Empress holds a sheaf of corn representing fertility and her role as Demeter, protector of the harvest. The red, heart-shaped shield shows her warmth and love, and the protection she gives nature. It also bears the astrological sign of Venus. The pomegranates on her robe, a fruit known for its quality as an aphrodisiac, suggest fertility, and emphasise her fecundity and sexuality.

Meaning

Not surprisingly, the Empress brings fertility and protection to a reading – a happy life full of home comforts and security. In general, this card promotes health, fertility, and richness to all with whom she involves herself, but care must be taken not to overuse her resources.

Reversed Meaning

When reversed the card may show a wasting of ability. It also indicates health problems, often infertility or difficulty in having children. This could be causing psychological problems that need to be resolved. Often the card in this position shows the person has lost the security of home life and longs to regain it. Someone who needs to learn caution or he or she will tend to continually overspend.

Astrological Influence

Venus

IV
THE EMPEROR

THE EMPEROR

If the Empress was mother goddess, The Emperor is the patriarchal god. His number, four, represents thought, memory, justice, and wisdom.

The Emperor's crown conveys royal status and possibly pagan lineage; pagan priests used to wear horns and crowns were a development of this headgear.

The Emperor is Cernunnos or Zeus, father of the nation. It was thought that the royal family had a divine right to rule; many rulers were worshipped as gods. Invalids were given the "royal touch", as it was thought that a king or queen could achieve miraculous cures.

Zeus was known to the Romans as Jupiter, and the card obviously has Jupiter as its ruling planet. The sign Leo also represents leadership and logical reasoning.

The Emperor's throne, a symbol of wealth, power and responsibility, is decorated with Aries, which, along with his sword, represents the influence of the Fire signs and the willingness of the Emperor to fight for his country and his beliefs. The Emperor holds a scepter topped by a solar cross, signifying male potency and his vigilant authority and protection of his domain. In his cupped left hand he holds a golden orb, suggesting his rationality; he rules by law rather than by brute force. Around him are the orange and red hues indicating fire signs. The tall, rugged rocks in the background emphasize the Emperor's steadfastness, while the stream at the bottom of the mountain shows his inner wisdom and deep understanding.

Some cards depict the Emperor with a shield or a crown decorated with an eagle, this symbolizes alertness, the forces of nature, the fire signs, and strength; many nations have used an eagle on their flags.

Meaning

The Emperor card shows determination and paternal authority. It indicates that the person is acting responsibly and is able to move forward, perhaps to take on a position of responsibility and authority. The card might also signify that the person fears the action of someone above him or her at work or, if connected with family matters, would show that he or she fears the responsibility of parenthood. In all, the Emperor brings leadership ability and courage, but also brings responsibility and the willingness to help others and take on their problems. It is a card of courage and stamina.

Reversed Meaning

The Emperor card reversed could signify that the person is acting immaturely and should heed the advice of an older person, perhaps a father. It shows that the person is insensitive and overbearing.

Astrological Influence

Aries

V
THE HIEROPHANT

THE HIEROPHANT

Also known as the High Priest or Pope, this card represents moral law and the wisdom of a spiritual teacher. The Hierophant can represent Zeus from a much more spiritual side than the Emperor.

In occult groups, the High Priest guards the implements, the mundane day-to-day running of the coven, while the High Priestess is the spiritual leader.

Zeus denotes a supreme god with the power to absolve humans from their sins. Zeus could only be approached through his high priests, an idea echoed in Christianity. The Hierophant's long staff, known as the Keys of St Peter, can bless, curse, bind, or loosen a person from his or her past misdeeds.

With the number five, he represents religion and theology and the ability to teach them.

The astrological influences are Pisces because this card represents spirituality, and the sun, the god force. The Hierophant pairs with the High Priestess who is the moon.

The Hierophant sits between two pillars, symbolizing the church or temple from which he rules. His right hand gives the sign of benediction. The card depicts a silver, lunar disc fastening his cloak, symbolizing unity with the High Priestess. This is a magical bonding and emphasizes the old idea that a loved one wears a token of the partnership: men would take a piece of their partner's clothing into battle for good luck.

The Hierophant's cloak is red, symbolizing his role as High Priest. The two keys at the bottom of the cloak represent the duality of nature: the gold key represents the sun god, the conscious mind, the silver key the moon goddess, the subconscious mind.

Meaning

The Hierophant card shows that the person is finding help with spiritual questions. The card suggests realization of one's own abilities and that hope stems from faith in those abilities.

It is a card of magic that can be summed up in an old saying from witchcraft, "To know, to dare, to will, to keep silence."

Reversed Meaning

When reversed, the card shows the person has looked deeply into a problem and is making a lot of effort to understand it. However, the person's soul-searching may be misguided; he or she needs to seek the advice of other people, otherwise mistakes will be made. The seeker has acted carelessly and has not taken the advice of those who have been willing to help.

Astrological Influence

Taurus

VI
THE LOVERS

Lovers in mythology are always two deities, such as Venus and Cupid, or Aphrodite and Eros. Venus is another mother goddess, and goddess of marriage. Eros, or Cupid, is the harbinger of love. In medieval Tarot decks, Eros appears in the Lovers hovering over a young man and two or three women, the man apparently trying to choose between them. This recalls the judgment of Paris, who died after becoming involved with judging a beauty contest between the gods, emphasizing that in matters of love, decisions are extremely difficult and should not be based merely on physical attraction. Modern decks usually have a naked couple, representing Adam and Eve in the Garden of Eden.

The Lovers are number six, representing harmony and love. The card is Gemini because of the two people, but Venus, signifying love, and Pisces, representing the spiritual, have more in common with this card as a card of spiritual love. The emphasis in this card is on spiritual love; showing that love can be between various people, not necessarily just a physical activity between couples. Keep this in mind when giving readings.

The bounteous growth on the trees represents love, common to all nature. Purity of love is shown on some cards by five white lilies – five being the number of creative thought.

It is a card of choice, perhaps not as eventful as the choice for Paris. Any loving relationship brings a lot of difficult choices and decisions. It is a card that shows the need to find mutual respect and individuality within a partnership.

Meaning

The Lovers can show anything from a new partnership to something much deeper. The wish is to be happy, to get on, to love, and to be loved.

The Lovers represents our need for companionship; consequently, this card is one of the most important of the Major Arcana. This card does not represent a shallow affection; it is about people's hearts and souls.

If the card is the right way up, the person may not be worried about love; they may have come for a different reason, and this should be addressed.

Reversed Meaning

If the card is reversed, it shows that the person has a lot of worries about relationships. It could also indicate a selfish attitude, in that the person wants only adoration from others, or a person who tends to want to receive more than he or she gives. As always, the cards positioned around the Lovers must be taken into consideration.

Astrological Influence

Gemini

VII
THE CHARIOT

The Chariot is a card of force and strength. Being number seven, it also represents security and safety. The Mars influence is obvious, the Cancerian influence of protection is represented by its symbol on the rider's belt.

In early decks the card represented victory, and had a female rider. The figure in the Chariot represents Mars, Ares to the Greeks, and to the Vikings Tui, as in Tuesday. In India he was Jagganatha riding his mighty chariot, Juggernaut.

The charioteer controls a pair of sphinxes, one black and one white, representing the positive and negative forces of life. The sphinxes are trying to go in different directions, and if he doesn't control them disaster will result. The forces of good and evil are battling to take the soul of the soldier.

The charioteer wears a crown of pentacles, the magic symbol representing man in microcosm. The symbols of the moon represent the water influence, as do the green tunic and the blue curtains. The moon is also a psychic barrier, as the charioteer tries to cut himself off from others around him. This card is about emotion, including anger; one of the strongest emotions that we can feel.

The scepter, and the emblems on his belt and tunic, show that he is very receptive to psychic forces. The charioteer must use his inner willpower to progress spiritually. The scepter also indicates his position of authority. The wheels of the chariot may represent the never-ending circle of life. The Chariot is not only a card of force and strength but, as its numerical value is seven, it also represents security and safety.

Meaning

The Chariot suggests the seeker has taken up some project or has difficult choices ahead on a physical or emotional level. He or she needs reassurance that the course chosen is the right one.

The seeker should watch the actions of others, who may regard him or her as strong-willed and courageous, but want the seeker to change course. The person can and must resist.

In all, the Chariot shows a person in control of his or her own life and destiny. The charioteer knows that there is no security in life without strength.

Reversed Meaning

The Chariot reversed suggests the seeker has been tempted from his or her path and needs to be shown the way back; lack of concentration and determination have put the seeker in severe difficulties. The card in this position shows that the person is liable to give in to the pressures of others, which would be detrimental in the long term.

Astrological Influence

Cancer

VIII
STRENGTH

Strength, also known as Fortitude, shows a woman holding shut the jaws of a lion, as in the medieval image of Cyrene, the nymph, wrestling, unarmed, with a lion watched by Apollo, who then fell in love with her. The woman uses the combined forces of mental and physical strength to subdue the lion. The flowers in her hair show the earth mother principle and the card accentuates the beauty and the beast image evident in so many of our folktales.

Some Tarot decks have Strength depicted as Hercules fighting a lion; others show Samson. It represents man as a species trying to control his animal instincts. Traditionally, the sublimation of sexuality was considered a virtue. In medieval occult lore, chastity brought with it the magical ability to control wild beasts. In the legend of the unicorn the only person who could catch the unicorn was a chaste maiden.

The lion and the unicorn often appear together. The lion represents the aggressive fiery force of the sun. The unicorn (sometimes also a deer) represents the feminine lunar elements.

Astrologically, Strength is represented by Mars, showing courage and energy. There is also a feminine Libran side that adds a gentle touch. The white dress that she wears shows her purity. The trees in the background indicate fecundity.

Strength in numerology is represented by the number eight, which signifies rhythm and balance, the ability to judge and to understand.

Meaning

The Strength card indicates the person is going through a time when he or she needs to gather great strength and willpower in order to achieve their objectives. Self-assured, the seeker will have the willpower to come through.

Strength is about inner strength, the willpower that you seem to be able to draw up when all the chips are down. It is a card of courage and resolve.

Reversed Meaning

When reversed, the Strength card can show illhealth as well as succumbing to the actions of others just because that is an easy option. It can show that the person is going through emotional stress and mental problems that have, perhaps, left him or her feeling listless. The person needs to learn that to maintain health there needs to be a balance between physical and mental capacity.

The seeker fears choking under too much pressure from others and that, physically, he or she will be unable to endure the pressure.

Astrological Influence

Leo

IX
THE HERMIT

The Hermit, or the Old Man in Italian decks, is identified with Saturn, the god of old age and wisdom. The Greeks new him as Kronow, meaning time. Saturn is also associated with agriculture as the reaper, since Saturn comes from "sator", meaning someone who sows seed. In many of the older decks, he is actually featured as Father Time, with an hourglass instead of a lantern.

The Hermit has Saturn and Virgo as astrological influences. The Hermit is a person searching for perfection and self-realization. Its number nine shows the attainment of goals and fulfillment, the foundation of a new cycle and phase before moving on to a higher level of understanding.

The Hermit stands on top of a snow-covered rock, representing solitary exile and loneliness. A lantern shows his way forward. Here is the light of knowledge that he strives for; the pentacle of Solomon inside the lantern represents wisdom. In some decks the lantern is an hour glass, showing that he represents time.

The cloak of the Hermit is of simple

linen, referring to his humbleness and to earth, which is the Virgo element. The cloak is also a symbol of protection from outside forces and his withdrawal from the world; keeping his thoughts to himself. Modern psychologists have found that being alone for extended periods of time often causes visions and revelations.

Meaning

The Hermit is someone developing awareness by abandoning materialistic trappings. The Hermit knows that deep within his or her own mind dwell the answers being sought. The card shows that this is a time for soulsearching and, perhaps, there is a need to take a step aside to plan. What is important is to listen to one's own intuition and the seeker is doing this.

The Hermit is the side of us that needs occasional solitude in order to be able to work out our thoughts. However, it is the card of a teacher, showing that we must not completely remove ourselves. If we are not there to help others, they will, in turn, not be there to help us.

Reversed Meaning

When reversed the Hermit shows a closed, stubborn mind that will cause disaster if the advice of others is refused. An extremely selfish attitude will lead to the person's undoing. Like Strength, there is a health element here, and it may show that the person is depressed and is cut off from others.

Astrological Influence

Virgo

X

WHEEL OF FORTUNE

WHEEL of FORTUNE

This is the card of fate. The Wheel of Fortune was a medieval game in which people bet on where a revolving wheel marked with numbers would stop. From this game emerged the modern roulette table.

There are several versions of this card. In some decks three people are pictured; the three fates or Moirai, and the three aspects of the moon: new, full, and dark, or virgin, mother, and hag. The spinning wheel has long been associated with witchcraft. The Wheel of Fortune derives from the spinning wheel because the Moirai were always pictured as spinners of destiny. In some decks the hand of fate comes out of a billowing cloud to turn the wheel, possibly belonging to Janus, the two-headed Roman god who guarded the doors of fate. Wind is associated with uncontrollable forces – no one can control their destiny. Janus gave his name to January, the new year, a time when people look to the future. In many decks the Wheel of Fortune depicts four animals representing the four seasons, the four fixed signs of the zodiac, and the elements – earth, air, water and fire. The snake represents the Egyptian god of evil, Set; the sphinx symbolizes resurrection; and the man-jackal suggests Anubis, the Egyptian god who led the souls of the dead away to be judged. The wheel is decorated with alchemical symbols and at the compass points letters that spell TORA or TARO. The numerological values of the Wheel of Fortune are 10 and one (1 + 0 = 1). One represents independence and 10 the beginning and the end, fate and completion.

The Wheel of Fortune has links with astrology; groups of planets circling around the earth govern luck and disaster. The Wheel could represent the zodiac, and the birth chart could be a person's individual wheel of fortune. It is under Jupiter's influence, the planet that governs financial luck. There is also a link with the second house of the chart as this rules money matters. It also has a Gemini influence; Gemini, like luck, is a two-faced sign and can be for or against you. Luck is thought to run in cycles, hence the wheel. Some decks feature a king and queen perched on the wheel to show that no one can avoid fate, whatever their status.

Meaning

The card can indicate change and luck. Generally, when upright it denotes good luck. It can also indicate change ahead; the seeker has to be sure to take advantage of certain conditions in order for things to work out favorably. It is a card of change; look at the other cards placed around the Wheel to see what areas of life are affected.

Reversed Meaning

When reversed the card denotes bad luck. Disaster is ahead unless the seeker is careful. It may be that someone is changing the pattern of life for the seeker, and that he or she should beware of others.

Astrological Influence

Jupiter

XI

JUSTICE

Justice is often personified by a woman holding scales, as in icons like the Statue of Liberty and the statue at the Old Bailey in London. The use of scales recalls ancient Egyptian symbolizm; after death the soul went to the Halls of Amenti to be weighed on the scales of Ma'at. The soul of the person was balanced against a feather of truth to determine if the person should go to heaven or hell. The scales of justice also tip to and fro during a person's life, so this card is also a card of luck and change.

In astrology the card is represented by Libra, depicted as a pair of scales. Because this sign is halfway through the astrological year it balances out the zodiac.

Justice sits on a throne representing the law of the land. She holds another symbol of authority, the sword, which is double-edged to cut through all situations without preference. The square emblems on her crown and her cape symbolize logical measurement, however, the circle inside the square represents the ability to use intuition. Many older decks show a knight positioned behind

Justice and may indicate carrying out justice on behalf of someone else. Justice represents the law of the land and the fact that no one can escape it in the long run; one day we will all be judged for our actions. Justice has a numerological value of 11, which breaks down to number two (1 + 1 = 2), which equals knowledge and balance.

Meaning

The Justice card suggests that the seeker has just come through a time that required looking very objectively and honestly at his or her ideas. The effect is beneficial, luck will be in the person's favor, particularly concerning legal matters. The card means what it says – Justice – so it might not always be in the seeker's favor. It is a card that warns the seeker to seek the advice of others when he or she needs it.

Reversed Meaning

When reversed the card suggests bad judgment in the seeker's plans, possibly from being too selfrighteous and not listening to advice, particularly from those in authority or those able to be objective. Unless there are a lot of changes made by the person, things are liable to fall flat. The seeker should be very careful when making any decisions and should heed legal advice.

Astrological Influence

Libra

XII

THE HANGED MAN

This card, along with Death, is one of the most feared cards in the pack. This fear is based upon a misconception, since both cards have positive aspects to them.

The Hanged Man represents Dionysus. In Greece, images of Dionysus were hung upside down in trees to bring fertility to crops. Gradually, the figure in the Tarot came to take on the image of Judas; some designs even have the figure dropping bags of blood money, received as payment for betraying Jesus. Hanging upside down was a form of punishment reserved for debtors. Later this method of punishment was used for traitors.

The image also relates to the initiation period of Masonic orders. Initiates were left hanging from a tree by their feet to meditate. Thus, the Hanged Man symbolizes the death and rebirth that the initiates had to go through.

In numerology The Hanged Man is twelve, a three number ($12 = 1 + 2 = 3$), representing creation and the development of the soul.

Astrologically, this card has a strong

Piscean influence, as this is the sign that embodies spiritual matters. Pisces also rules the twelfth house – twelve being the number of the card – the house of self-sacrifice and self-undoing. Saturn has its influence, accentuating self-sacrifice, anxiety, and depression, which this card can point out.

The figure hangs from a tree, tied by his right foot. His left foot forms a cross with his leg, suggesting spiritual crucifixion. The red of his trousers and belt represent man's instinctively passionate nature and his occult wisdom. The blue tunic represents intuition; this card is very much about the use and misuse of intuition.

Meaning

Spiritual awareness is the message of this card. Whenever it appears in the pack it shows a need to reevaluate the current situation. The seeker is going through selfanalysis and needs to use intuition. Other people find the seeker hard to understand and solitary in his or her actions. This is the card of self-sacrifice, someone who puts others first. A constant worrier, not sure of what to do, when to do it, and how others will react.

Reversed Meaning

A reversed Hanged Man indicates the person needs to unscramble his or her thoughts, and is, perhaps, experiencing severe mental depression. The seeker's aloofness and depression frighten others away from giving desperately needed help.

Astrological Influence

Neptune

XIII

DEATH

DEATH

Death is the most feared Tarot card, but without justification. The card represents transformation rather than death. Anyone scared of one card should consider not using the Tarot.

Death is often pictured as a skeleton with a scythe – the skeleton being all that remains after death, the Scythe a symbol of Saturn the reaper, whether of corn or souls. Some decks picture him on horseback as the Angel of Death slaying all in his way. Death, like Saturn, is associated with time and fate; the word mort, from where we get mortuary, comes from the Moirai, the three sisters of fate.

Another influence is Scorpio, the eighth house, the house of the occult, the unknown, and reproductive organs. Sex, or its representation, plays an important role in many occult rituals.

Thirteen is a significant influence. Jesus had twelve disciples, Judas being the unlucky thirteenth. Thirteen was lucky in pagan beliefs because there were supposed to be thirteen witches in a coven. Thirteen has the numerical influence of four (13 = 1 + 3 = 4), representing measurement, time, and logical thinking.

Black armor shields the mysteries of death, representing the negative sides of life, against the purity and beauty of the white rose, representing the immortality and freedom of the soul. Some decks show the heads of royalty and peasants on the ground, indicating that death transcends status. The setting sun represents the soul; both will rise again, though in a different guise. The red river is the river Styx that the dead have to cross on their way to the underworld.

Meaning

This card is not about physical death; other cards have more to do with that. It is a card of transformation, the death of the old self and birth of a new person. It indicates the person has made drastic changes to his or her life and needs to start afresh and leave the past behind.

The person may feel a need to learn about reincarnation; life after death. The card indicates someone preferring continuous change, with no commitment to the past.

The Death card is unavoidable in one form or another. It indicates a time for new roles and regeneration. Welcome the changes – refuse them and they will be forced upon you.

Reversed Meaning

When reversed, the card could show changes that were forced by events, possibly the death of someone has made the seeker look more to the future. It may indicate someone without commitment to past activities.

Astrological Influence

Scorpio

XIV

TEMPERANCE

The design of Temperance is medieval. He is a mysterious figure, some think he is Ganymede, a Trojan prince abducted by Zeus to fill his cup with the juice of immortality. Another correlation is with Aquarius, the eleventh sign of the Zodiac, known as the water bearer. Like all Tarot history, this card has a mixture of origins.

The numerological influence is five (14 = 1 + 4 = 5), which is the number of change and lack of stability.

The figure of Temperance is an androgynous angel – balancing the male and female spirit. Temperance represents Lucifer, the light-bringer, as indicated by the halo.

The red triangle indicates the fire signs, the blue robes purity, also reflected in the water the figure pours and at his feet. Water flowing from cup to cup represents the stream of ideas between conscious and subconscious, the higher thought of humankind and the need for spiritual regeneration onto a higher plane. The figure stands with one foot in and one foot out of the water, looking perfectly balanced although the foot in the water is not touching the bottom. This represents standing with one foot on the reality of earth and one foot in the subconscious. The wings of the angel represent spirituality, movement, and communication. A yellow light in the distance refers to the wisdom to be found if you dare to walk up the long, winding road. The flowering irises represent radiance, another about to bud, represents promise. The lush growth indicates fertility.

Meaning

The Temperance card suggests the seeker has to make a choice. Perhaps this person started something part-time that has begun to take over his or her life. The seeker does not know whether to commit fully. He or she may be going through change from a practical to a more spiritual situation.

The seeker hopes to carry on two projects simultaneously, fearing having to make a final decision. It is a card of evenhandedness and diplomacy. Weighing the options, being guided by the spiritual in preference to the material, but ideally aiming to balance the two, so that they mutually support and encourage.

Reversed Meaning

The person must be very careful. Things are very unstable, and if they are not sorted out very carefully everything is liable to collapse. Shows that the person is preoccupied with the material side of life; his or her ideas are bound to fail.

Astrological Influence

Sagittarius

XV
THE DEVIL

The Major Arcana are linked in pairs, the opposites, Devil and Temperance, a prominent example. This card, like Death, is much maligned.

The Tarot Devil is a medieval image, with a demonic goat's head, often with bat wings and a trident or flaming torch. The evil goat head with glaring, almost hypnotic eyes represents the goat god of pagan beliefs, and the Greek god Pan. His horns are twisted indicating his mind is also. Above him an inverted pentagram signifies the negative aspects of magic. Some decks show a candle, signifying the essence of life; the flame is weak and the candle has almost burnt out portraying the Devil's ability to snuff out the life force. His evil is sometimes indicated by a fly, representing Beelzebub, the Lord of the Flies. Some cards have a red circle in the background indicating intense emotion and aggression.

The astrological influences of the card are Saturn and Capricorn, since Capricorn is the sign of the goat, and Saturn its ruler.

The numerical influence is six

($15 = 1 + 5 = 6$). This is a number of acceptance and satisfaction, seemingly an odd number for the Devil, but actually well suited. The number of the beast, as stated in Revelations, is 666.

Meaning

The Devil card indicates the person should be very careful in the future. He or she is being materialistic and may be excessively under the influence of others. Although quite happy to be in this situation, it will work against him or her eventually. The person can and should make changes in his or her life. Though unwilling to do anything about a problem, other people realize the person is capable of solving it. Others may feel the person acts like an indulgent tyrant. The Devil can show excessive concern with sexual conquest. The Devil is a card of temptation, acting as a warning to the seeker. If attitudes are not changed immediately it may soon be too late.

Reversed Meaning

When reversed, the card is even stronger and can mean that the person has no option and must adapt to fate in the best way possible. This can show the unbalanced mind of a depraved person. It also warns of the depraved actions of others that, while accepted, may not be good for the seeker.

Astrological Influence

Capricorn

XVI
THE TOWER

THE TOWER

The Tower is sometimes known as The Lightning-struck Tower or *La Maison Dieu*, The House of God. However, some old decks used the word *diefel* (devil) rather than *dieu*, making this the House of the Devil, or hell. Another old name for this card is the Hospital or Hostelry, perhaps borne of the idea that the dead were meant to be guests of the god of the underworld. The Italian Bambi deck titles this card The Castle of Pluto.

The number of the Tower is sixteen or seven ($16 = 1 + 6 = 7$), numerologically a magic number, the number of occult learning and soul development. It is a card of rising out of the flames like a phoenix, and going through a ritual rebirth in life.

This card has a lot of Mars influence, not just in the force and strength, there is also courage, hope, and willingness.

The Tower is sturdy, with firm foundations that should be able to survive attack from outside. However, the flames, caused by the lightning, are gutting the building, forcing those inside to jump into the rough waters where, probably, they will drown.

Meaning

All the elements of this card, and their bleakness, point to destruction – but it is a card that relies on the strength of the foundations of the seeker to determine how he or she will cope. This card shows that the seeker is going through a very destructive phase in life, an aspect that perhaps needs to be swept into the past. The person may not have planned things well. Although this is a traumatic time, he or she will be able to start anew. It represents a change in the old values, but out of this comes hope.

The person needs to tread very carefully, otherwise destruction could also mean ruin. The Tower shows that the seeker will go through a time of sudden inspiration and traumatic change that cannot be avoided. This card brings new hope and awareness, providing the seeker's thoughts and motivations are built on firm foundations.

Reversed Meaning

If this card is reversed, then the problem has come about by the seeker's own negligence, and it is going to take a while, if not a very long time, to put things right. Through lack of objectivity they will lose the opportunity to change.

Astrological Influence

Mars

XVII
THE STAR

The Star represents Venus, the goddess, and the brightest planet known to the ancients. The picture also represents Aquarius and perhaps the mother goddess in her virgin role in the three developments linked to the moon's phases: that is the virgin for the new moon, the mother for the full moon, and the hag for the waning moon. The mother goddess is sometimes known as Astrea, meaning star, from whom, mythologically, life was poured into the barren planet Earth. Sirius, thought to one of the largest stars, was the most important star in Egyptian mythology, and many people today believe it is inhabited by beings that have visited Earth.

This card has also been linked with the Star of Bethlehem as the star of salvation and renewal.

Numerologically, it stands for eight (17 = 1 + 7 = 8), the number of regeneration, hope, and reward. A card that signifies rebirth.

The female is nude, symbolizing her freedom and abandonment of the fetters of society. Her blonde hair, along with the clear water, represents the purity of her thoughts and eternal life. The water also indicates a fertile life and the forces of nature.

The red bird, flower, and pitcher represent emotions and mental activity, while the blue pitcher represents the subconscious mind. After the shattering, traumatic experience of the Tower, new hope is born.

Meaning

Fresh inspiration leads to success and so this card shows that the seeker has a wonderful opportunity for rectifying mistakes. The seeker, though possibly hesitant, needs to make use of the opportunities around. A very optimistic person with a lot of hope for the future, and as long as this state of mind is maintained, success will result. In all, this is a card of hope and optimism, bringing new insight and happiness and a message of help to those who are willing to try. It signifies a rebirth of the seeker's ideals, and the efforts of someone willing to make his or her future clearer.

Reversed Meaning

In the reversed position, the Star usually signifies someone who has been overly optimistic, which will lead to disaster. It can also show someone who is going through emotional problems and taking an overly pessimistic attitude toward life. The person needs to boost self-confidence, otherwise wishes and goals will wither.

Astrological Influence

Aquarius

XVIII

THE MOON

With the Moon we must consider the aspects of the three phases: the thin white crescent of the new moon, associated with the Virgin, Persephone; the full moon, represented by the Mother Goddess, Isis; and the waning moon, depicted by the Hag, such as Hecate.

The moon rules the tides and, by its influence over the tides, the seas. This adds to its magical qualities. Given that water is the major component in our makeup, we, too, are affected by the moon.

It has the numerological influence of nine (18 = 1 + 8 = 9), showing completion of a cycle and the start of a new phase. In astrology, the Moon rules Cancer; in the Tarot Pisces also has an influence. This can be seen, at the bottom of the card, by the crayfish, originally a crab, that rises out of the pool of the subconscious, linking it to water. A wolf and a dog howl at the Moon, showing that this card rules our animal instincts. On either side of the card are towers, shown on some decks as one round and one square, which perhaps represent the pillars of Jachin and Boez in the tree of life. Others believe that they may represent the pillars of Hercules that stood at the exit of the Straits of Gibraltar, guarding the way to the magical land behind the North Wind, Britain.

Many older designs show dewdrops coming from the Moon signifying its astrological influence on us. A twisting path leads the way through the hills. The Moon, then, is the card of intuition and subconscious instinct.

Meaning

The Moon indicates that the seeker is in a state of confusion and feels compelled to follow his or her intuition but has been reluctant to do so, as it does not seem practical. This card often comes up when someone is thinking of writing a book or taking up art as a fulltime occupation.

The seeker should rely on his or her intuition; by following his or her instinct, the seeker will be successful.

It is a card about intuition, thoughts, and emotions. When reversed, these can become overwhelming and lead to depression, but when the right way up these feelings lead to a greater understanding of life.

Reversed Meaning

Reversed, the Moon indicates illusion; the seeker has been daydreaming about plans and needs to look at things more practically. Muddled plans can lead to disaster.

Astrological Influence

Pisces

XIX
THE SUN

The Sun is a giver of life, and of fire. To light the tinders at the major festivals, such as Beltane and Halloween, magical bonfires would be made by focusing the sun's rays through a piece of glass. Fire was associated with purification; from this came the ritual of jumping over bonfires as a means of warding off evil influences.

The sun brings the summer while the moon rules winter. The birth date of the sun god, known also as Mithras, was December 25, as after this date the sun became warmer and the days became longer. This is another example of a Christian festival imposed on a pagan festival.

Numerologically, the Sun is represented by one ($19 = 1 + 9 = 10 = 1 + 0 = 1$), the start of a new period. As the Moon is the end of a phase, so the Sun is the beginning.

In astrology, this card is ruled by the sun and Gemini, as the couple pictured in the cards originally represented the Gemini twins of Castor and Pollux. This card has the Arian qualities of strength and action.

Nowadays, many Tarot cards picture a male or female youth, representing the different aspects of each other and the duality of the sign. The colors of the card are orange, gold, and yellow, signifying the card's rule over gold, and showing the warmth of the card. The golden hair of the child pertains to the sun's rays, as do the sunflowers that always turn their heads towards the sun. A brick wall behind the horse and child signifies security and foundation.

Meaning

The Sun indicates hope and pleasure for the future. Health and happiness are accentuated in this card. The seeker desires happiness and security out of life and is willing to work toward that goal. It is a card of achievement. A card that holds strong, positive rewards for effort. Whereas the Moon points to spiritual and emotional success, the Sun points to material success, but only through work.

With both the Moon and the Sun cards, it is important to remember that they represent different aspects of the same creative force of life. You cannot have one without the other.

Reversed Meaning

The Sun reversed could indicate possible disaster through broken contracts and overoptimism. It shows a person who is not going to put in the effort needed to get the result, possibly leading to disaster.

Astrological Influence

Sun

XX

JUDGMENT

Judgment is also known as Resurrection. It often depicts an angel appearing over tombs from which naked bodies are rising. In this deck, Saint Michael, the Christian version of Mercury, awakener of the dead, blows the trumpet that heralds the last judgment. The cross on the flag attached to the trumpet is his emblem. A naked man, woman, and child rise from the grave in the card, their spiritual souls to be judged, not their outward position in life (signified by clothing). They represent a family unit, the female and male aspects of life, and the union of the two, the child representing the reconciliation of these forces. The bodies rise out of the grave, signifying rebirth, the blue color pointing out that this is a spiritual, not physical, redemption. Some decks show the trumpet of glory and liberation sounding the last judgment, coming from a cloud covered with fire, bringing a fire element into this water card.

This card represents resurrection, whether it be a spiritual resurrection of the initiate, or the resurrection of

Dionysius or Jesus. It also signifies judgment from God, the weighing of merits on the scales of life and the principle of Karma. The belief in Karma permeates the Tarot, and to fully understand the Tarot an acceptance of reincarnation is helpful.

Numerologically, this is a card of two $(20 = 2 + 0 = 2)$, bringing knowledge, the balancing and weighing of the positive and negative forces of life.

In astrology, the card bears the influence of Pluto and Scorpio. Mercury, which is a very similar planet to Pluto as far as astrology is concerned, also has an influence here.

Meaning
This card represents the final examination of the consciousness and, therefore, is associated with self-awareness. It has a very spiritual connection. However, it is a time when the seeker should look inward and determine whether an answer is truly desired, for its dictates will demand a lot of effort. Usually this card is positive.

Reversed Meaning
When reversed Judgment can signify that the seeker has never accepted the answer. It also signifies a lost soul.

Astrological Influence
Pluto

XXI

THE WORLD

The final card of the Major Arcana is the World, sometimes known as the Universe. The card usually depicts a naked woman within a victor's wreath. At the corners are four heads – a lion, bull, man, and eagle.

These four faces represent the four elements: the bull of Taurus (earth), the lion of Leo (fire), the eagle representing Scorpio (water), and the man representing Aquarius (air). The four faces also represent the seasons and the Christian Gospels.

In the center is a female covered by a free-flowing scarf and holding two batons (or magic wands). Around her is the ancient victor's wreath. The magic wands symbolize power. The robe draped around her is in the ruling color of purple. The wreath not only symbolizes victory, but also the circular nature of the universe and all its cycles. Often, in the background there are tiny stars, representing the vast unknown of the Universe. The figure is the initiate in the new role, reborn and ready to start the cycle again. The Fool has become master. However, with the ending of each cycle a new one begins.

Numerologically, this is number three ($21 = 2 + 1 = 3$) and is the development of one and two to bring about creation and birth. In astrology, this is a card of Saturn, with a strong Taurean influence.

This is the card of the final goal, being one with God and eternal life after Death, the beginning of the new cycle.

Meaning

The card represents results and a feeling of completion. Hence, when this card appears at position one in the Celtic Cross spread it indicates the start of a new journey. It can show that others are looking up to the seeker as a teacher and guide, which must be taken into account when he or she analyzes future actions.

Reversed Meaning

When reversed it tends to show a more materialistic viewpoint of someone who is overly content with his or her own world and needs to explore outward, and consequently, their inner mind. It can mean that others cannot reach the seeker and that he or she needs to open up and share knowledge.

Astrological Influence

Saturn

THE MINOR ARCANA –
CARD BY CARD

THE FOUR SUITS IN OUTLINE

Swords

Fire. Active, energetic, determined, dynamic, achievement-oriented, ambitious. Needs perpetual movement to feel alive. Ruthless, insensitive, volatile, angry. Inclined to naiveté. Flamboyant, extroverted, demanding of attention. Power-seeking.

Astrological signs: Aries, Leo and Sagittarius.

Pentacles

Earth. Passive, static, unyielding, possessive, rich. Pentacles pertain to the material world and to concepts of value. Once possessions have been painfully acquired by slow toil, there is a reluctance to give them up. Tradition, pragmatism, and dislike of change. Scientific objectivity and a tendency to categorize, to "take stock." The passion of the collector, antiquarian.

Astrological signs: Taurus, Virgo and Capricorn.

Wands

Air. Active, intangible, hot and cold, mental. The realm of the intellect and its products: reason and imagination. Functions through communication – words, signs, abstractions. Generates ideas, theories, plans (which are realized by Swords or Pentacles). Exercises discrimination and worships logic. Tolerance, open-mindedness, progressive attitude, and detachment.

Astrological signs: Gemini, Libra and Aquarius.

Cups

Water. Passive, mutable, dissolving, feeling, maternal. Cups represent the emotional environment – the power of understanding through intuition, sympathy, and empathy. Functions by relating and responding to instinctual urges. Expresses an emotional spectrum from love to hate. Feminine, caring, nurturing. Adapts to the mood of the moment. Exudes passion, sensitivity, romance.

Astrological signs: Cancer, Pisces and Scorpio.

Feeling For Meanings

The meanings of the cards in the suits that follow are not exhaustive. You will pick up your own feelings in the cards and allow your intuition to come through as you become more skilled. Meanings must always be adapted to suit the nature of the question. For example, the Five of Cups – basically the card of romantic infidelity and separation – in a spread relating to a career query, is more likely to indicate the dissolution of a financial partnership than the seeker's, or anyone else's, imminent divorce.

THE SUIT OF SWORDS

ACE OF SWORDS

Description – A hand in the sky holds a sword decorated with a crown, palm leaf and olive branch.

Meaning – The sword relates to fire, and this card suggests vitality, victory, a completion of one's ideas and triumphs in projects. Whereas wands represent the emotional or spiritual, the swords are definitely much more physical and tend to be related to work.

Reversed meaning – This can mean plans or projects are delayed and that the subject must struggle with problems.

TWO OF SWORDS

Description – A blindfolded young woman sits by a seashore holding two swords in her crossed hands.

Meaning – The seeker does not know which way to turn, feels blindfolded and has a difficult choice to make. This is a time for clear thinking but making a decision is difficult. The seeker should not rush to come to a decision or randomly commit.

Reversed meaning – Wrong decisions are easily made: the person has a tendency to rush, to take the first course of action without considering the consequences. The card suggests taking advice from friends, but eventually the seeker alone must decide.

THREE OF SWORDS

Description – A heart is pierced by three swords, clouds behind the heart discharge heavy rain.

Meaning – The meaning of this card is fairly obvious: a broken heart, grief, and sorrow. However, the sun can be seen behind the heart, indicating that the grief, sorrow and hurt can be put in the past. Behind every cloud there is a silver lining. Overcoming the fear of immobility.

Reversed meaning – Depression and sorrow have been with the subject for some time, and he or she has found it very difficult to recover. This card typically represents a relationship in the distant past from which the subject never recovered. Until resolved, the subject will never be truly happy in any new relationship.

FOUR OF SWORDS

Description – A Knight is lying on a tomb in a church. Three swords are above and one below him.

Meaning – This card indicates worries and possibly depression. The seeker may need to take time to retreat from the world to clarify his or her direction. This card also represents the stage between finishing training and embarking on a new adventure. Putting theory and skills into practice.

Reversed meaning – Can indicate ill health. May also indicate that there are immense pressures upon the person that cannot be ignored.

FIVE OF SWORDS

Description – A man holds three swords in the foreground. In the background two figures seem to be mourning by the shore. The sky is wild and ominous.

Meaning – Beware of the actions of others. A time not to be selfish, but the seeker should make sure that he or she is aware of and in control of all situations.

Reversed meaning – The subject could find him or herself hurt by other people. Someone may make changes to the subject's career about which he or she will not feel happy and which could threaten his or her responsibility.

SIX OF SWORDS

Description – A woman and child are being ferried across the Styx, the mythological river separating heaven from earth. Six swords are in front of them.

Meaning – A card of mourning and grief, often reluctantly leaving a life behind and starting on a new course. It can also mean a physical move, but always having to leave something behind in order to move on. Lacking the desire to go on.

Reversed meaning – This means the seeker hasn't started the journey to leave something in the past, but this will happen. The seeker may have been putting the journey off, therefore life is in turmoil as he or she does not know in which direction to turn. A need to hasten making decisions to achieve a better environment.

Seven of Swords

Description – A man is creeping away with five swords; two remain stuck in the ground.

Meaning – Pressures of work and life are upon the seeker but it is necessary to push on. The load may be too heavy, making it necessary to leave some things behind and not take on so much. However, if the seeker perseveres he or she will reach the desired destination. There is no use in dwelling on past mistakes.

Reversed meaning – The pressure may be overwhelming and the seeker has collapsed under it. He or she needs to let go to save what strength remains – a need to relax away from an overly stressful job.

Eight of Swords

Description – A woman, surrounded by swords, is blindfolded and bound in front of a castle on a hill.

Meaning – This is typically the card of someone tied to the home or the house and family. Only the seeker can untie the ropes. There is no magic wand. Though it may be difficult to untie them, bit by bit the seeker can loosen the restrictions and feel more comfortable. The card suggests someone who has ideas but is tied and needs to cut him or herself free.

Reversed meaning – Can represent someone that continually puts him or herself into the same detrimental situation and then is bound by it, such as a woman who is battered who either keeps going back to same man or keeps getting into similar relationships.

NINE OF SWORDS

Description – A woman sits up in bed holding her head, nine swords hang horizontally above her.

Meaning – This card has similar meaning to the eight; being tied down, but it also suggests plans and projects and the feeling that energy is repressed. Again, only the seeker can break him or herself free. The positive aspect is that what stifles the seeker is in sight, with perseverance, aims will be fulfilled. The seeker is acting for the common good, not personal gain.

Reversed meaning – Other people are pressurizing or tying him or her down. It can mean the seeker is putting too much pressure on others. A time to consider helping or receiving help from others.

TEN OF SWORDS

Description – A man lies on the ground with ten swords bloodily piercing his back.

Meaning – Obviously, this card represents being stabbed in the back. This is, therefore, a time to watch others carefully. The seeker must beware of others plans and actions as they could be ruinous to him or her. Someone could out-manoeuver the seeker in work or another role. The seeker should avoid revealing plans or ideas to others who may steal them.

Reversed meaning – The seeker should be careful to be fair with other people and should not take advantage. The card suggests pursuing a vocation he or she has been considering. A requirement to defend others and ensure those less fortunate are being protected.

PAGE OF SWORDS

Description– A fair-haired youth with a sword looks ahead. Red clouds are forming in the sky.

Meaning – This is a card of youthful energy, a card of passion. Someone beginning a quest or the start of a plan but perhaps lacking some discipline. If not steadied, the person may find that some of his or her plans do not lead to fruition. This card suggests making sure ones energy is properly directed.

Reversed meaning – In the reversed position this card indicates someone who starts something but never finishes. Greater perseverance and channeling of thoughts is required.

KNIGHT OF SWORDS

Description – A dark Knight on horseback, dressed in armour, charges forward holding a sword aloft. The sky is slashed with windswept clouds.

Meaning – A battle is in progress, and there is a need to be courageous. The seeker aims to be successful in his or her plans and ambitions.

Reversed meaning – This card is heightened in a reversed position. It indicates someone who will stop at nothing – including selfishness – to achieve the desired end. If the person carries on unchecked in this way, he or she will end up seriously upsetting friends.

QUEEN OF SWORDS

Description – A woman sits on a throne holding a sword in one hand and jesturing with the other.

Meaning – This card suggests roses: pretty to look at, sweet-smelling, beautiful flowers used to represent love but, down their stems are sharp thorns. This is the card of someone who can make him or herself out to be a rose, kind and loving when showered with love but also selfish when he or she wants to be. This person is well able to protect self from others.

Reversed meaning – The reversed meaning shows spiteful or malicious gossip about the seeker. Can suggest selfishness to an extreme.

KING OF SWORDS

Description – A serious-looking man holding a sword, sits on a throne and stares directly ahead.

Meaning – The subject is a mature person who has achieved career satisfaction and found purpose in life. This is someone able to make decisions, a skilled speaker, politician and diplomat. A strong leader who is able to determine whether strength or tact is required in a given situation. Someone who is generally comfortable with their life.

Reversed meaning – In a reversed position this card indicates that the subject is resentful of what he or she has not achieved and can be selfish, abusive of power, and overly authoritarian. Some would consider this card the signifier of a politician.

THE SUIT OF PENTACLES

ACE OF PENTACLES

Description – A hand in the air holds a pentacle. An arch in a garden hedge reveals distant mountains.

Meaning – This card indicates happiness through financial stability, wealth or career progression. Certainly financial good news or a golden opportunity.

Reversed meaning – Financial stability is sought; the card indicates an opportunity that will ensure this will soon appear and should be seized.

TWO OF PENTACLES

Description – A young man is balancing two large pentacles, behind him is a very choppy sea with two boats riding the waves.

Meaning – This is a time of balancing books, weighing choices, reflecting on a career and trying to create greater harmony in work. It shows a decision or choice in work or career needs to be made. A good time for thinking about contracts.

Reversed meaning – Problems with finances, instability. It is no use running away from financial problems. It is time to figure out how to balance a budget.

Three of Pentacles

Description – Early Success – A craftsman is being watched while he attends to an ornamental column in a doorway decorated with three pentacles.

Meaning – This card represents learning a trade. With hard work, rewards will eventually come to the apprentice. Skill and craftsmanship.

Reversed meaning – Reversed, this card still represents the apprentice. The subject is unsure of his or her role, if the right career choice has been made. Additional effort is required to achieve desired goals.

Four of Pentacles

Description – A content but alert man sits with four pentacles, there is a town in the background.

Meaning – Concentration in money matters is required at this time; it is also a good time for thinking about long-term stability and for making decisions about buying a house or changing jobs.

Reversed meaning – Although this is a good time, it is also important to read the small print carefully and be alert to any possible problems. Urgent and sudden house expenses may arise.

FIVE OF PENTACLES

Description – An impoverished man and woman walk in snow outside a building with a stained-glass window depicting five pentacles.

Meaning – This card shows the need to help other people. It indicates financial problems and can often represent the seeker giving help to others or requesting help from people around him or her. This is a time for sorting out financial problems.

Reversed meaning – In the reversed position this card indicates the seeker must take advice from other people as the financial situation and strife around him or her have become overwhelming.

SIX OF PENTACLES

Description – A wealthy man is shown standing with a set of scales in his left hand and money in his right hand which he appears to be handing to other people.

Meaning – This card indicates success in legal matters and that it is now a particularly strong time for looking at contracts and dealing with taxes. There may be a tax rebate coming.

Reversed meaning – In a reversed position this card could indicate that money will have to be paid out to resolve a legal issue or contract. This is not a good time for entering into any financial transactions.

SEVEN OF PENTACLES

Description – A man stands with a hoe in front of large bushes covered in pentacles.

Meaning – This is the card of reward. It represents seizing opportunities, putting in the required effort, and reaping rewards. From little acorns oaks grow.

Reversed meaning – In a reversed position, however, this card indicates that the seeker is unsure of his or her direction in life or is wasting effort in the wrong arena. It can also indicate that the person started something but did not carry it through, thus needs to try harder. The seeker is not making sufficient effort to get what he or she wants.

EIGHT OF PENTACLES

Description – A craftsman is working hard at creating pentacles, examples hang on the tree beside him.

Meaning – The seeker is a patient, skillful person who puts forth much effort. He or she has artistic skills, and is, perhaps, looking for artistic expression rather than simply financial reward, though financial success will result to a certain extent. The seeker will gain artistic acceptance but must be careful not to compromise his or her talents.

Reversed meaning – It is important to concentrate on details, as this card shows someone who rushes and does not take enough care, someone who is apt to start a project but may not carry it through.

Nine of Pentacles

Description – A woman, whose attire indicates wealth, holds a falcon in her left hand. The bushes around her are covered with pentacles.

Meaning – This is a card of financial success, of material attainment and happiness, but it can also represent materialism at its worst; rigidly seeing everything only in terms of commercial value.

Reversed meaning – The subject is not comfortable with his or her surroundings. Although possibly financially and materially secure, he or she feels dissatisfied and is longing to try something new.

Ten of Pentacles

Description – An affluent elderly gentleman sits surrounded by his family, dogs and property.

Meaning – Another card that represents contracts, particularly those that deal with home and the long-term future. It also indicates that this is a good time for entering into legal partnerships.

Reversed meaning – Be wary of contracts and divorces that could be costly. Financial problems could cause a lot of disruption to the home and family.

PAGE OF PENTACLES

PAGE of PENTACLES

Description – A young man holds up a pentacle. There are trees and a lake in the background.

Meaning – The subject has had a secure upbringing, thus has confidence and strong opinions, and ideas of where he or she wants to go in life. This is a scholarly person who has decided on a career.

Reversed meaning – The subject has a strong financial base, home, and family life but, illogically, throws it all away. The seeker wants to escape the past but because of his or her background this is unrealistic, and certainly illogical as far as relatives and family are concerned.

KNIGHT OF PENTACLES

KNIGHT of PENTACLES

Description – A Knight on his horse gazes towards the distance. He has oak leaves on his helmet.

Meaning – Another card indicating a seeker who has focused goals and is able to carry them through. This is a mature person who thinks deeply and is practical. This is a good time to start new business endeavours and to make financial commitments. Without prompt action the opportunity will be lost.

Reversed meaning – This card suggests the person is extremely practical and efficient but, for some reason, never completes his or her ideas. The person is always losing out because he or she keeps putting off decisions to take action on potentially successful ventures.

QUEEN OF PENTACLES

Description – A mature woman sits on a throne on a hills. Oak branches surround her.

Meaning – This is an intelligent and elegant person who feels financially secure, and will do anything to protect that environment. This is someone who shields self from problems behind a hard exterior.

Reversed meaning – This person is unwilling to face the severe financial problem he or she has and is trying to pretend it does not exist by putting up a false front. This card indicates stubbornness and willpower at their worst. It can also indicate that the seeker is trying to control his or her children.

KING OF PENTACLES

Description – A young King sits in lavish surroundings on a throne decorated with bulls' heads. There are grapevines and various golden ornaments.

Meaning – This is the card of the shrewd businessperson, the entrepreneurial type who is practical, determined, hard headed, strong and careful but still willing to take on challenges. This person is also protective but not generous.

Reversed meaning – In this position the card shows a corrupt individual who abuses control and dominates other people, who enjoys the finer things in life but does not earn them through his or her hard work. This card can indicate self-inflicted financial ruin.

THE SUIT OF WANDS

ACE OF WANDS

Description – A hand holding onto a wand appears out of clouds above a castle and trees.

Meaning – Wands represent ideas and the Ace represents, depending on its position in a layout, either the beginning or culmination of a new opportunity or idea. A card of mental stimulation and taking action. Generally, all the Ace cards in the Tarot can represent the beginning or the end of opportunity.

Reversed meaning – Obstacles, delays, lack of progress. The subject feels weighed down by the responsibility of decisions and struggles in an oppressive cloud of ignorance, before finding a way out.

TWO OF WANDS

Description – A man appears to be looking into a globe of the world as though it were a crystal ball.

Meaning – The start of studies, the possibility of starting a journey, usually a mental one. However, depending on the layout, this card may also indicate that it is a good time for communicating with other people, particularly those a long distance away.

Reversed meaning – Delays, obstacles placed in front of the seeker, difficulties focusing on studies and a strong need for perseverance. The seeker cannot "see the wood for trees".

THREE OF WANDS

Description – A man wearing a cloak and cap, and flanked by wands, stands looking over a lake.

Meaning – Just as the two represented someone starting their course of action, the three represents someone who is already halfway there. This is a more mature person who tends to be connected with business opportunities rather than studies, but the persons plans are temporarily stalled. The person must be willing to accept help from others. This is a time for taking advice.

Reversed meaning – Be careful of others; do not sign agreements at this time. Generally not a good time to enter into partnerships. Progress comes under attack from others.

FOUR OF WANDS

Description – In front of a castle, four wands are linked by a flowers, suggesting a triumphal arch. A couple approach it, each with bouquets held aloft.

Meaning – This is a card of the home, a card of celebration, of thoughts connected with home and family life. It represents a mentally secure time when the seeker feels happy about his or her life and home situation.

Reversed meaning – Problems around the home that need to be addressed. It is a time for looking at how others feel about the seeker and their relationship to him or her.

FIVE OF WANDS

Description – Five people are battling against each other with wands. Each of them is wearing different colors and appear to be of a different race.

Meaning – This is a card of struggle, of opposition and competition. It indicates a need for great perseverance, a time of pushing through obstacles to eventually rise above the problems. Success that wins respect and admiration from others; rising in status.

Reversed meaning – Problem with agreements, contracts. Not a good time to enter into partnerships. A time to think very carefully before signing any legal documents.

SIX OF WANDS

Description – A soldier sits on a horse surrounded by wands. He is wearing a victor's wreath on his head and another decorates the wand that he holds.

Meaning – The seeker will be successful in converting his or her ideas into action. The wands behind the horse indicate that it is a good time to present ideas to others as they will be convinced of their worth.

Reversed meaning – The seeker must be careful not to overestimate his or her own abilities and needs to be sure to consider other people's plans and thoughts. If the seeker neglects this he or she risks losing their support.

SEVEN OF WANDS

Description – A young man appears to be winning as he fights off six wands that seem to be threatening him, with his own wand.

Meaning – With strength, mental perseverance and courage, the seeker will overcome the obstacles he or she is facing. A time to push forward with ideas, not a time to give up.

Reversed meaning – Indicates a need for caution. The seeker should not try to take on too much at any one time. A need to take help from others, not to go it alone.

EIGHT OF WANDS

Description – Eight wands are flying through a clear blue sky. A river runs through the peaceful landscape below.

Meaning – This card suggests thoughts of travel and of a journey. It is a card of fast movement, particularly air travel, with other people. At its most mundane it can mean a vacation, at its most important a relocation of the family. This card is associated with enjoyment. It also represents news and communications from others.

Reversed meaning – Delays or cancellation of travel plans or other arrangements.

NINE OF WANDS

Description – A man holds a wand. He is standing in front of eight other wands. His head is bandaged and he appears to be ready to defend his position.

Meaning – The seeker is pleased about his or her current life situation. This is a time for feeling happy about one's work environment and mental state. This card also indicates the possibility of new challenges, a promotion or other new prospects. This is a time for looking forward, seizing opportunities.

Reversed meaning – Reversed, this card suggests career uncertainty and unsettled feelings about where one's life is headed.

TEN OF WANDS

Description – A laborer is carrying ten wands with some difficulty.

Meaning – The card indicates that the seeker is facing a very difficult time and that great perseverance is necessary. At times the difficulties will feel almost too great, but with tenacity he or she will overcome them. This will not be an easy task.

Reversed meaning – Reversed, this card shows that the difficulty the seeker is facing feels almost insurmountable and that he or she is likely to succumb to the temptation to give up too soon. An even stronger need to battle on, not to give up on ideas.

PAGE OF WANDS

Description – A young man looks at a wand as if surveying an area of land with it.

Meaning – This card shows a young person surveying the future, looking for direction in life. It is typically the card of the young student, a person who needs to make up his or her mind. The mountains in the distance suggest that these are long-term plans or long term ideas.

Reversed meaning – Reversed, this card usually suggests a young person lacking or plans or forethought and is easily influenced. Someone who needs to sort out his or her life.

KNIGHT OF WANDS

Description – The Knight of Wands brandishes his wand from the sadle of his galloping horse.

Meaning – This card signifies a person facing opportunity. Unlike the Page whose opportunities were somewhat distant, here they are imminent and will need to be seized shortly .

Reversed meaning – A need for caution and careful planning. The seeker should not rush ahead with the first idea that comes to mind.

QUEEN OF WANDS

Description – A noble Queen is wearing a crown adorned with flowers symbolising fertility. She is holding a wand in one hand; in the other hand a large sunflower that reaches up to her shoulder.

Meaning – This card can represent a proud parent. It shows a patient person willing to help others. The sunflower represents the seeker's ideas and the need for sustained growth and cultivation of ideas.

Reversed meaning – Reversed, this card shows mistrust of someone else's ideas, even jealousy. If this card appears in a relationship, it can mean the two people have difficulty explaining their ideas to each other, or have different ideas of where they want to go in life.

KING OF WANDS

Description – A mature King wearing a cloak sits upon a throne decorated with lions and salamanders. He looks ahead with determination. The crown is an ornamental headpiece that represents ideas.

Meaning – This card represents a mature, intelligent, and educated person, a strong father figure at ease with himself and the family around him. This is a leader, someone with the ability to impart knowledge and ideas to other people. A respected teacher.

Reversed meaning – In the reversed position this card indicates an overly severe person who acts before thinking, and can be very disapproving if someone else's ideas do not match his or her own.

THE SUIT OF CUPS

ACE OF CUPS

Description – A hand holds forth a cup overflowing with water. A dove with outstretched wings is above the cup. Below the cup are a bed of lilies and a poppy head. The cup represents the element water.

Meaning – This is a card of immense joy and in particular, shows love and happiness in relationships and all spiritual matters. Meeting, receptivity, responsiveness, warmth and romance.

Reversed meaning – Loss of love, relationship, stalemate in a relationship, and a need for reevaluation of ideas and spiritual requirements. It can also indicate infatuation.

TWO OF CUPS

Description – A young man and a young woman gaze deeply into each others' eyes, each holding a cup towards the other.

Meaning – This is a card of mutual, exclusive love between two people. Can indicate the start of a new relationship or love affair. Fun, good company.

Reversed meaning – This usually means stagnation, difficulties in relationships or a delayed relationship. A time to talk to others or the partner about the relationship. Restraint, uncertainty, and lack of commitment. Insecurity.

THREE OF CUPS

Description – Three women are dancing, they wear garlands in their hair and each holds up a cup in a gesture of celebration. Fruit and flowers are strewn on the ground at their feet.

Meaning – This card indicates great happiness and joy, often associated with a celebration or party. A time to communicate with other people in a social situation. Coming together, marriage, compatibility.

Reversed meaning – Reversed, this card indicates delays to plans, problems with family, particularly in-laws.

FOUR OF CUPS

Description – A figure by a tree, reminiscent of the green god of pagan mythology or the Jack-in-the-Green from Morris dancing, looks at a cup being offered to him by a hand coming out of a cloud.

Meaning – This is a card of great, typically unexpected opportunities, providing much emotional support and satisfaction. It is also a card of strong spiritual opportunity, learning and knowledge.

Reversed meaning – When reversed, this card shows that opportunities are likely to be missed. It also indicates a time when the seeker is meant to help someone else.

FIVE OF CUPS

Description – A man in a black cloak looks down at some wine spilt from three goblets. He has not seen the two that are still standing. In the distance, across a river, is a ruined castle.

Meaning – This is a card of sadness, crying over spilled milk. The seeker should forget problems of the past and start again with what remains. Loss of trust and love.

Reversed meaning – Reversed this card has a similar meaning. It represents a time of patching up misunderstandings with other people, of helping others through relationship problems. In all positions, it represents being able to put the past behind.

SIX OF CUPS

Description – Two children are looking at each other over a cup of flowers. In the foreground are additional cups filled with flowers.

Meaning – This is a time of happiness and family. Obviously, this card is about children and can indicate anything to do with them, including news of pregnancy or birth. It also indicates an innocent state of mind and approach to life.

Reversed meaning – It can show problems with children, or, indeed, if it relates to the seeker, it indicates an unwillingness to accept of the issues around him or her. A fear of growing up and tackling problems.

SEVEN OF CUPS

Description – Seven cups containing various objects float in the clouds. Someone below looks up at them.

Meaning – This is a card of tremendous choices, almost too many. It indicates that the person needs to think about what he or she wants and is indicative of wonderful new horizons. When making choices the person must avoid spreading him or herself too thin.

Reversed meaning – This is the card of the seven deadly sins, to which the images relate. Rather than wonderful opportunities, reversed, this card suggests a selfish hedonist; an excessive person burning the candle at both ends. The seeker needs to concentrate on the spiritual, rather than physical pleasures in life.

EIGHT OF CUPS

Description – A cloaked man is heading up a path by a river which is edged with steep-sided rocks. Eight cups are arranged symmetrically behind him. It is night and there is a strange moon with a face.

Meaning – This card represents personal effort that will lead to success. It is a solitary card, indicating some loneliness in any project or relationship. It also represents disappointment in love and relationships and a time to journey on to something new.

Reversed meaning – A need to seek emotional stability. A need for the seeker to sort out his or her problems, to sit down with another person and express feelings, to overcome a difficulty in communicating with others.

NINE OF CUPS

Description – Nine cups surround a wealthy, slightly inebriated, man who appears happy and joyous. He is rather plump, representing a Falstaffian figure.

Meaning – This card represents self satisfaction, happiness with position and environment, a person enjoying life in general. It is symbolic of a very happy and fulfilled period of time.

Reversed meaning – Reversed, the card can signify gluttony and over indulgence. Typically, it can indicate problems with health due to over-eating, alcohol abuse, or even allergies to certain foods, particularly shellfish.

TEN OF CUPS

Description – A couple gesture at a rainbow in the sky, with ten cups in front of it. Two children dance beside them.

Meaning – Typically this is a card of engagement, marriage, happiness in a relationship. There is much love and trust in this position.

Reversed meaning – Reversed, this card signifies difficulties in relationships, unhappiness and quarrels, but like all reversed cards, it can indicate problems that have been overcome.

PAGE OF CUPS

Description – A young man, slightly effeminate, wearing a large billowing hat, stares dreamily into a cup with a fish in it.

Meaning – This is a card of strong meditative thoughts and spiritual longing. This card indicates someone with artistic gifts and strong spiritual ideas. Typically, it represents someone who needs to express him or herself spiritually and artistically.

Reversed meaning – In a reversed position, this card can indicate that the seeker is having difficulty coming to terms with his or her sexuality or sexual feelings. It may represent a slightly lazy person who never puts into action his or her ideas and artistic aspirations.

KNIGHT OF CUPS

Description – A Knight in armour with wings attached to his helmet holds a cup and looks toward the wooded hills.

Meaning – This card represents someone with a strong spiritual understanding and a more mature artistic sensibility than the Page. Suggests someone who has won a spiritual quest, someone who is at a pivotal point in his or her life.

Reversed meaning – Reversed, this card represents someone whose heart rules his or her head and who may make promises related to emotional matters that he or she cannot follow through.

Queen of Cups

Description – A woman with fair, braided hair holds an ornate cup. She sits in a throne by the sea.

Meaning – Astrologically, there is a lot of Venus and Cancerian influence in this card – it is a card of emotions and feeling. It signifies someone with strong compassion and feelings. It highlights family influences and can represent matters concerning family and children.

Reversed meaning – Reversed, it can indicate problems with childbirth. It represents depression, moodiness, and feelings of emotional unhappiness.

King of Cups

Description – A fair-skinned King holding a scepter and a cup sits on a throne, apparently on the sea.

Meaning – This represents a person with a strong ability to advise others, a person who has completed his or her artistic or spiritual journey, who is generous with his or her empathy and understanding.

Reversed meaning – It can represent someone who thinks he or she has reached their goals or fulfilled ambitions, but who actually has not, or vice-versa. It can also show someone who is emotionally selfish and thinks only of him or herself. This person may even show a tendency toward emotional blackmail.

Placing and Reading the Cards

Always begin a session by putting the client at ease and tuning into his or her character by reading what is known as a character spread. During this first reading, clients will begin to recognize themselves, which strengthens their faith in your abilities.

Obviously, seekers are only going to believe in your reading if you have started off by telling them some truths about their character and past.

The Astrological Circle

One of the best spreads for this initial reading is what is known as the astrological circle. Lay twelve cards out in a circle corresponding to the houses in astrology and lay one card in the center for luck.

First house corresponds to the ascendant in astrology, and indicates the seeker's general personality.

Second house relates to financial matters and security.

Third house relates to communications and how someone communicates with others.

Fourth house relates to home environment, and family.

Fifth house relates to creativity, children, and artistry.

Sixth house relates to work and health.

Seventh house deals with romance, love, marriage, and partnerships.

Eighth house is the house of occult, death, inner feelings, emotions, and legacies.

Ninth house represents travel, education, and interests.

Tenth house relates to careers and ambitions.

Eleventh house deals with friendships and how the person relates to others.

Twelfth house deals with subconscious, and repressed feelings and is associated with Karma.

Thirteenth card, in the center, relates to hopes and future wishes.

Reading One

Jenny, a woman in her mid-thirties, has come for a reading.

The cards drawn were as follows:

1 Queen of Wands

2 Knight of Pentacles reversed

3 Page of Swords

4 Seven of Swords

5 Seven of Wands

6 Nine of Pentacles

7 King of Swords

8 The Moon reversed

9 The World

10 The Hierophant

11 Three of Swords

12 Nine of Swords

13 King of Pentacles

First is the Queen of Wands, signifying that Jenny is intelligent, an academic person, someone who uses her mind and studies hard to achieve what she wants. She is someone with a strong need to find things out for herself, who is interested in reading books and writing. The client confirmed this in that she had been to university and was at the time embarking on a new career in journalism.

In the **second position**, is the Knight of Pentacles reversed. The second house relates to finance and in it this card reversed indicates financial problems and often that plans have been difficult to carry out because of financial problems caused by others in the past. It also shows someone who has her own ideas about what she wants to do in the future. The seeker confirmed that this was true in that she wanted to set up a business but couldn't because of financial problems caused by a breakup with a boyfriend.

In the **third position**, which relates to communication, is the Page of Swords, a card of communication. This suggests someone who is able to put plans in motion, who is able to inspire others to practical action. Taken in conjunction with the previous cards, we gradually get a sense of someone who is full of ideas but better at promoting other people rather than herself.

In the **fourth position**, the house of home and upbringing, is the Seven of Swords. This indicates someone who has felt lonely and put upon in her home life, who has felt that it has been one long trial. The client confirmed that due to a parental split, she had been left to care for her mother and younger sister.

The **fifth position** is the house of family and tends to relate to present circumstances. The card here is the Seven of Wands, which shows that she still feels burdened by her family, but she is willing to face that challenge. The seeker is someone who is able to persevere and move gradually forward although her life isn't easy.

In the **sixth position**, which is the house of work and health, the seeker had the Nine of Pentacles. This means that generally she is a healthy person but that she needs to watch for overindulgence and maybe even food allergies. Jenny confirmed that she was generally healthy but often suffered from gastric problems and was forced to avoid certain foods that tended to heighten the problem.

The **seventh position** is the house of relationships and love, and here is the King of Swords, which indicates that the client is attracted to very strong people, men of action and strength, but that she also needs someone who is very loyal and protective.

In the **eighth position** is the Moon in a reversed position, which indicates a deep psychic ability that perhaps will remain hidden for a number of years. Being reversed suggests a tendency toward depression and a feeling that the world is against her. This card could also show difficulties in relating thoughts and emotions to those around her.

In the **ninth position**, which in the astrological order is called the house of travel and journeys, is the World. This indicates someone who has a great desire to travel and who enjoys learning about new cultures. Coupled with the previous cards, this shows someone who has a strong interest in ancient beliefs and archaeology and is able to absorb a lot of information.

In the **tenth position**, is the Hierophant. This suggests that the seeker is ideally suited to a career in which she would give advice to others – even advice of a spiritual nature. She would work well in any counselling position. The client confirmed that she had worked as a psychologist and was involved in teaching psychology.

The **eleventh house** is the house of friendship. The card here is the Three of Swords, indicating sorrow and pain and a feeling of being let down. However, the client should remain calm because, behind the sorrow, is light. Although she has been let down she must not think that she should give up on involvement with friends or groups. The client confirmed that a person who she thought was a friend had spread a rumour that had deeply hurt her, making her think about rejecting that circle of friends.

In the **twelfth position** is the Nine of Swords. This indicates the feeling of being tied down to others' wishes and not being able to take control of her own life. The client is the only one who can make the decision to cut herself free.

The **thirteenth card** represents hope, wishes, and fulfillment. In this reading it is the King of Pentacles, indicating that the seeker has a need for financial security and independence that will allow her to really take control of her life and do the things that she wants to without having to rely on others.

Reading Two

A young woman, Sarah, came for a reading. Again the astrological houses were used. *The cards drawn were as follows:*

1 Five of Wands	8 The Hermit
2 Seven of Pentacles	9 Five of Swords
3 Six of Wands	10 Judgment
4 Eight of Cups	11 Seven of Swords
5 King of Pentacles reversed	12 Seven of Cups
6 Ace of Pentacles	13 The Fool
7 Seven of Pentacles	

In the **first position**, the Five of Wands implies that the client has strong willpower and determination and can battle through all odds to achieve what she wants.

In the **second position** is the Seven of Pentacles, which indicates that she is not afraid to work hard to receive the rewards that she desires.

In **third position**, the house of communication, the Six of Wands indicates a loyal person who has great ability to teach others, and to communicate and take control of situations.

In the **fourth position** is the Eight of Cups. This indicates that there have been a lot of problems around the home, which Sarah confirmed. The problems that she had in her relationship with her parents had affected the way that she had entered into subsequent relationships. She, therefore, needed to be able to put the problems

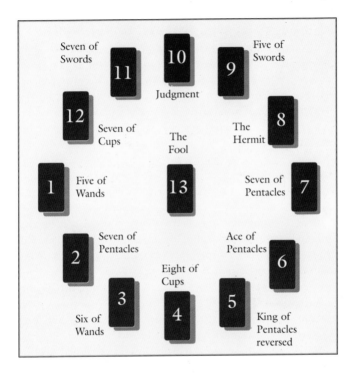

and the situation behind her.

In the **fifth position** is the King of Pentacles reversed, which again indicates problems with family circumstances, but also indicates that the seeker is likely to pull out of relationships before making a commitment.

In the **sixth position** is the Ace of Pentacles which shows a hard-working person willing to give support and help other people as well as help herself.

In the **seventh position** is the Seven of Pentacles, which in this case, reading from the rest of the cards, indicates that in a relationship she ended up supporting the other person more than they supported her.

In the **eighth position** is the Hermit, which indicates that she hides her feelings from others, keeping them very much to herself. It also suggests that she needs a lot of space and wants to hide inside her thoughts. This presents problems when she needs to explain her feelings in a relationship.

In the **ninth position** is the Five of Swords, which indicates that she has not achieved her goals and has regrets about travel and studies. Sarah confirmed that she wished she had gone to university when she had the opportunity.

In the **tenth position** is the card of Judgment, which indicates that Sarah is very adaptable to new work situations and has recently discovered a work environment in which she would like to find a job.

In the **eleventh house** is the Seven of Swords, which indicates that she is often carrying burdens for friends and that she tends to be used for support by others. She, perhaps, now needs to think of herself and push on in her own direction.

In the **twelfth** is the Seven of Cups. Undeniably, her biggest problem was a fear of having to make a decision or choose a path. She is like a person confronted with a range of ice-creams who does not buy any because she cannot decide on one flavour. Sarah acknowledged that she found it difficult to make up her mind in relationships and work situations. She regretted this in many ways as she felt that decisions she had avoided in the past had led her into her present situation, in which she wasn't happy.

In the **thirteenth position** is the Fool, which indicates a positive new start in a new venture and the ability to learn to leave certain experiences behind. However, Sarah thought that there were still others around her trying to pull her from her chosen path.

The Celtic Cross Spread

This spread is one of the simplest, best known, and most useful. It can be used for a wide range of questions, from the yes/no variety to those with a more subtle psychological slant.

Some readers get the seeker to choose a significator – a card that represents them – out of the Court cards of the Tarot after they have shuffled the pack. This is not necessary – the choice is yours.

Each position has a predetermined meaning as listed below. There are several versions of the Celtic Cross, each with slightly different place interpretations; this is an effective variant.

The Meaning of Each Position

Card 1 – the seeker

The first card describes the person asking the question – perhaps adding some vital clue to his or her character, or attitude toward the question.

Card 2 – the question

This card throws light on the matter being considered. The cards listed below should be watched for. If they appear, give a cautious reply or redeal, according to your discretion.

Fool – wrong question, time, or wording. Seeker is confused.
Tower – brings disaster to whatever is planned.
Hanged Man – spread answers unvoiced, subconscious question.
Moon – issue clouded by secrecy or scandal.

Card 3 – the aim or desire of the seeker

This shows the ultimate wish of the seeker in the matter: his or her ideal, fantasy, ambition, where the seeker wants to go in life.

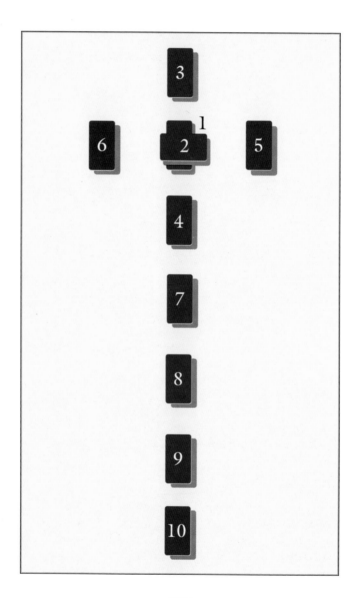

Card 4 – the root of the matter

Describes something about the origins or motivation impulse of the issue, such as distant events that have influenced the present and are still felt.

Card 5 – that which is behind the seeker

The recent past, prevailing current attitude towards the problem.

Card 6 – that which is before the seeker

What is likely to happen in the near future.

Card 7 – the seeker's best course of action

What the seeker can do to help him or herself towards a goal.

Card 8 – external influences

People whose circumstances could affect the outcome in a positive or negative way, and who may already be involved.

Card 9 – the seeker's emotions

Underlying feelings and attitudes towards the issue. Fears, suspicions, doubts, hopes, etc.

Card 10 – the final outcome

This card sums up the reading and provides the specific answer. Should this appear to contradict the rest of the reading, reconsider your approach to the question. Has personal bias affected your judgment?

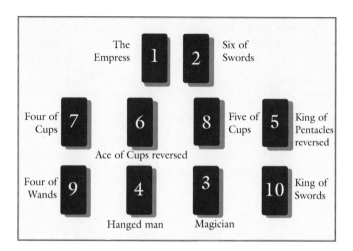

The Transformation

Once you have become accustomed to the basic moves of the spread it is a good idea to draw your assessment together and confirm the interpretation by looking at the linked pairs of cards. First, you move the cards into the pattern shown above, to make it easier for you to see the connections. The transformation also shows the client that something new is happening.

Each of these pairs has a logical bond and, if the cards are compatible, suggests that the reading has worked.

The seeker's action clearly can affect the near future and vice versa. (7 and 6)

External influences are usually already present, and may have played a role in building up the situation. (8 and 5)

The emotions tend to be linked to what the seeker sees as the origin of the problem. (9 and 4)

If the aim and outcome are harmonious you have a guarantee of success. (3 and 10)

To conclude, you can return to reevaluate the seeker and question cards in the light of the new understanding.

Reading Three

The Celtic Cross Spread, which is the most commonly used, allows a deeper look into Sarah's situation.
The cards drawn were as follows:

1 The Empress
2 Six of Swords
3 The Magician
4 The Hanged Man
5 King of Pentacles reversed

6 Ace of Cups reversed
7 Four of Pentacles
8 Five of Cups
9 Four of Wands
10 King of Swords

The Empress as the **first card** indicates that the root of the problem lies in emotions, relationships, long-term settlement, and family commitments.

In the **second position**, combined with the Empress, is the Six of Swords, a card of sorrow and mourning; certainly, in this case, indicative of the recent passing of an important relationship.

In the **third position** is the Magician, which indicates that Sarah wants to take control of her own life and not be manipulated by others. She also wants to develop her own skills.

In the **fourth position,** the root of the matter, is the Hanged Man, which indicates again the strong feelings and pressures that often cause Sarah to put herself in difficult positions. It also indicates that she is not at ease with herself mentally, feels that the world is on top of her and tends to become despondent. Life has been literally turned upside down.

In the **fifth position** is the King of Pentacles reversed, which indicates sudden changes in financial stability. Sarah confirmed that she had recently given up on a career path that she had been following.

In the **sixth position** is the Ace of Cups reversed, which suggests that the problems associated with the relationships around her are still not resolved, but that she needs to distance herself from them.

The **seventh position**, looking for the seeker's best course of action, is the Four of Pentacles. This suggests seeking stability in life, her need to start building security for her future and thinking of her long-term goals.

The **eighth position**, Five of Cups, shows the influences around Sarah, indicating that she needs to put the problems that she has been dealing with and other people's influence behind her so she can start anew.

The **ninth position**, the Four of Swords, indicates that Sarah is still very worried about what the future will bring.

In the **final outcome** – position ten – is the King of Swords, which indicates that perseverance and a fighting spirit will result in achievement and satisfaction.

When the transformation spread is formed it is apparent that the user needs to build her life, stick to what she believes in, and in particular, the emotions of nine and four need to be accepted but not allowed to be overly influential in her long-term objectives.

Reading Four

A middle-aged woman, Sally, came for a reading. She was particularly concerned about wanting to move. Again, the Celtic Cross Spread was used. *The cards drawn were as follows:*

1 The Fool

2 Ace of Pentacles

3 Two of Wands

4 Eight of Wands

5 Six of Cups

6 Ten of Wands

7 The Chariot reversed
8 Nine of Pentacles

9 Knight of Pentacles
10 Five of Pentacles

The **first card** drawn was the Fool, which represents the seeker. It is not a card that indicates Sally is searching for a new beginning, rather that she is wanting to leave the past and its circumstances behind.

In the **second position,** which represents the question, is the Ace of Pentacles, suggesting finances. Obviously, Sally will need to deal with financial issues if she wishes to move.

The **third position**, which is the seeker's aim, is held by the Two of Wands, indicating a need to look elsewhere. It shows Sally feels she has to move away to escape the sadness she feels at the moment.

The Eight of Wands in the **fourth position** suggests travel connected to a move in the past, either for a new or existing job. It appears that, emotionally, travelling was the wrong choice for Sally, and she now wants to return to where she started.

Sally also feels that she has left her family in the past, represented by the **fifth position** and the Six of Cups. There is a wish to regain the support and help of her family.

The **sixth position**, is the Ten of Wands, representing what lies ahead for her, does not show an immediate end to her problems; there is still a struggle ahead. There is also a need for perseverance.

In the **seventh position** is the Chariot reversed. This indicates that Sally has often felt that her life has been stretched in two different directions and that she has not been in control of it. Now is the time for her to take control of where she is going and decide what she wants to do.

The **eighth position** showing the Nine of Pentacles indicates that there are people around Sally to give her both emotional and financial support. This indicates that there are going to be people to help her; she will not have to rely solely on herself but she must have a course of action and be determined. Sally should write down and think about what she wants to do and then set her mind to achieving that end.

In the **ninth position**, is the Knight of Pentacles, which indicates Sally has ideas about what she wants to do but fears they will not come to fruition. She is worried about being trapped by her current circumstances.

The Five of Pentacles in the **tenth position** indicates that Sally needs to be available to support others in her family. Ultimately, she will be able to pursue her own wishes but she must be willing to support others in the meantime. Sally should not feel that she is being manipulated by everyone else. This is going to be very important at this time because she feels cut off from her family.

It is not going to be an easy few months for the seeker. The transformation spread shows the Chariot and the Ten of Wands grouped together, which indicates a struggle and a strong need for perseverance. It is important that Sally gets the support of family around her. They will become even more of an influence in the long term.

The Knight of Pentacles and the Eight of Wands grouped together also indicate that the problems originated in the past. As a result of moving to different places, Sally feels her ideas have never had enough time to develop, and she wants to do this now. But it is important that she understands her need to give support to other people as much as to herself.

The **final group** in the transformation, the Five of Pentacles and the Two of Wands, indicates Sally's ability to recognize a need to help and support others. She is able to look forward and see the best way to proceed.

In conclusion, Sally's anticipated move will take place so that she will be closer to her family, who will welcome her and require and appreciate the support she can offer them.

The Calendar Spread

Another useful layout is the Year Ahead, or Calendar Spread. Simply lay out twelve cards representing the months ahead and a thirteenth card to represent the year as a whole.

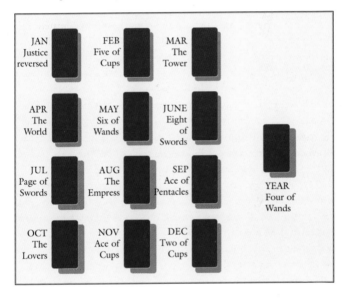

JAN Justice reversed	FEB Five of Cups	MAR The Tower	
APR The World	MAY Six of Wands	JUNE Eight of Swords	
JUL Page of Swords	AUG The Empress	SEP Ace of Pentacles	YEAR Four of Wands
OCT The Lovers	NOV Ace of Cups	DEC Two of Cups	

This reading has an advantage over many other spreads in that it can pinpoint the month in which certain things may occur and, by using your intuition combined with, perhaps, the numbers of the cards, you can often pick the exact date on which the influence starts.

Sometimes, though, you will notice that the meanings of two or more cards actually seem to melt into each other. This indicates a long-term or major change, such as a move, which would typically start in one month, when the house is put on the market but would not be completed until some months later when the person actually moves. This is also an excellent spread for answering questions about when will be a good time to move or change jobs.

Many people prefer to lay this spread out three cards at a time, rather than individually or all together. The advantages of this are twofold: if you lay cards out individually it is difficult to see a seasonal or long-term influence and, if you lay them all out at once, the seeker tends to be more concerned with a Death card or Tower shown nine months ahead than with what you are saying about the next couple of months.

Reading Five

The three cards drawn for January, February, and March are as follows:

Jan	Justice reversed
Feb	Five of Cups
Mar	The Tower

Justice reversed in January indicates matters in law going against the seeker. This could be a speeding fine or something more serious. In this case it is necessary to look to the cards that follow. Five of Cups in February indicates a need to look at disappointments. It is followed in March by the Tower, which represents a traumatic change; a decision, possibly legal or financial, goes against the seeker. As a result, they need to make a lot of changes, which may include a move. A typical scenario would be a house repossession. However, there is no such thing as fixed fate in the Tarot, so the seeker could be warned to adopt a different attitude, such as to deal with any legal matters very carefully and to take advice from others. He or she will then be able to make appropriate changes to avoid problems.

This is reflected in the cards for April, May, and June, which are:

April	The World
May	Six of Wands
June	Eight of Swords

The World in April indicates a feeling of fulfillment and relief, an opportunity for the seeker to put the past behind him or her and to take control of life. This is followed by the six of wands in May, which represents taking on new challenges, particularly in a work environment, and coming up with ideas that will be supported and followed by others. However, the Eight of Swords in June warns that the seeker may feel tied down; the execution of ideas may be delayed, but this is the time to persevere rather than withdraw.

Following on, for July, August, and September:

July	Page of Swords
August	The Empress
September	Ace of Pentacles

These three cards indicate that July, August and September will be more productive, happier months for the seeker. The Page of Swords in July represents dynamic energy, but the seeker must be careful not to be too impetuous.

The Empress in August indicates a fertile time, when many areas of the seeker's life will be happy and fulfilled. This is drawn onto September, represented by the Ace of Pentacles, which shows financial stability. The Empress in August can also mean news of fertility, often denoting pregnancy, but you would need to establish whether the seeker is questioning their work situation or their personal life.

The following three months, October, November, and December show:

October	The Lovers
November	Ace of Cups
December	Two of Cups

The meaning of the cards here is fairly obvious. An important relationship will start up in September and will lead to complete fulfilment and emotional happiness in the following two months and possibly a marriage or engagement in December.

Year card   Four of Wands

The card for the year is the Four of Wands, indicating a time of emotional security and looking and feeling happy. This card shows satisfaction in home life.

In general, this spread shows that the seeker will go through a distressing time with home matters early in the year but will be able to put this behind him or her and experience renewal. This will lead to emotional happiness and much more secure feelings about the future.

The Three-Card Spread

There will be occasions when using the other spreads, when the answer to a seeker's question may not be immediately evident in the cards that have been laid out. Generally, this happens with broader questions that require a very simple answer. There is no need to do a spread using many cards when all that is required is a simple yes or no answer, and possibly a little advice. The Three-Card Spread is ideal for this purpose.

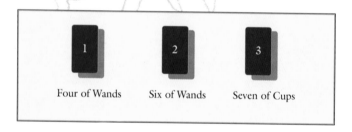

| Four of Wands | Six of Wands | Seven of Cups |

The deck is shuffled and three cards are laid out, the first representing the past, the second the present, and the third the future. Giving a reading with only a few cards is actually more difficult than giving a reading with lots of cards, for it relies much more heavily on the reader's psychic ability; the mind has to work harder to fill any gaps.

Reading Six

A young woman, Jo, is in a relationship and wants to know about the possibility of children in the near future.
The cards drawn were as follows:

1 Four of Wands
2 Six of Wands
3 Seven of Cups

The Four of Wands in the past indicates happiness; it could indicate marriage and happiness in the relationship. In the present position is the Six of Wands, the card of victory, indicating that it is a good time to go ahead with an idea. Indeed, the spread finishes with the Seven of Cups, which is the card of happiness and fertility. This reading would indicate that the time is right for Jo to plan a family.

Reading Seven

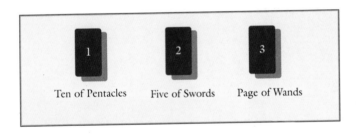

Ten of Pentacles   Five of Swords   Page of Wands

A young man, Jamie, wants to know whether he should take a job that he has been offered.
The cards drawn were as follows:

1 Ten of Pentacles   3 Page of Wands
2 Five of Swords

The Ten of Pentacles in the past suggests previous happiness within his work and other roles and indicates particularly good chances for long-term stability. The Five of Swords in this position indicates present worries and feelings of uncertainty. The Page of Wands suggests looking forward; Jamie now has to look toward his future and long-term plans, rather than at his past. Although he is content where he is, it will be far better for him to take action now lest risk never achieving the success and career progression that he desires.

The Name Spread

Readings in which you are asked to analyze seekers' problems are the most common, but on occasion a seeker may wants to know about potential employees.

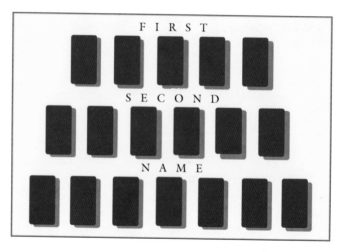

A useful spread in this case is the Name Spread. The layout consists of three rows of cards. The first line corresponds to the number of letters in the first or Christian name and represents the jobs the prospective employee has held in the past. If the person is known by an abbreviated name, for example Bill instead of William, just lay out the cards for the shortened name. The second row of cards is laid according to the letters in the middle name. If the person does not have a middle name, repeat the number of cards for the first name. This row of cards represents why the person wants to change jobs. The surname or family name will represent how the prospective employee will do in the future.

This is not to suggest that this should replace normal interview methods, but when there are two or three possible candidates, all apparently equally qualified, this spread is very efficient as it allows the seeker's deep intuition or gut feelings about the applicant to come to the surface. It has an advantage over astrology and palmistry as the employer does not need to ask the applicant for their time and place of birth, or to see their hands.

Reading Eight

The first thing to do is lay out the cards representing the first name of the candidate, in this case, Alan.
The cards drawn were as follows:

Knight of Swords reversed
The Star
Wheel of Fortune
Two of Cups

The Knight of Swords reversed indicates that Alan has shown drive and ambition in the past but has not always used them productively.

The Wheel of Fortune and the Star together indicate that Alan's career has gone through many changes, a process he has not enjoyed, although each time he changes jobs it is with hope and optimism.

The Two of Cups indicates that in the past his work has been significantly affected by relationship situations.

The next set of cards relate to his middle name, Paul.

The cards drawn were as follows:

Three of Cups
Five of Swords
Judgment
The Hermit

Again the cards should be read together.

The first card, the Three of Cups, indicates that family matters are a major concern; it may be that he wants a more secure future.

The Five of Swords and the Judgment card indicate that he wants to take control of his own life and make decisions for himself. The Hermit indicates that he is looking for a job that is more in tune with his inner feelings.

Overall, the cards indicate that he is returning to a job or something in his life that he had done before or started before. The cards also indicate that he is a bit of a loner and may find it hard to mix in with groups. He may be best in a job where he has to rely on his own initiative.

The last set of cards represent his surname, in this case Smith:
The cards drawn were as follows:

Seven of Swords
The Emperor
Seven of Cups reversed
The Fool
Seven of Wands

The Seven of Swords indicates that, initially, he will struggle in the job. However, he is a person of perseverance and providing he adapts himself to the changing circumstances, he has great potential.

The Emperor indicates strong leadership potential and loyalty.

The Seven of Cups reversed indicates that he may be prone to go down avenues that are not profitable for the company, and so would need to be guided.

The Fool indicates that this is a completely new start for Alan and that he would begin the job at a very basic skill level, strengthening the caution to the employer to monitor his actions closely during the first months of his employment.

The Seven of Wands indicates that he is someone of strong mind and willpower and that he will overcome adversities in the long term.

Overall, this reading suggests that it would take some time before Alan would become a profitable asset to the company but, if given time, he would eventually be very successful. If the employer were to hire Alan, he would be wise to put him on a fairly long probation period and to look at Alan as a long-term investment.

In this example, Alan was hired in a sales position, but it was nearly a year before he started earning a significant amount of money for the company.

The Tarot, of course, is not giving you a definite yes or no answer about whether the seeker should hire this person, for decisions cannot be abdicated to the Tarot. All the Tarot can do is show facets that may be hidden to the conscious mind. Ultimately, the decision has to be the seeker's, and like in most situations, there is always a positive and negative aspect to any answer.

Further reading

The books that follow have all influenced my ideas. To all, some degree of debt is owed. I apologize for any omissions.

Boak, Gerald	Prediction book of Taromancy, Javelin, UK, 1985
Butler, Bill	Dictionary of the Tarot, Schoken, US, 1975
Crowley, Alistair	The Book of Thoth, US, 1944
Dummett, Micheal	Game of the Tarot, Duckworth, UK, 1980
Douglas, Alfred	Tarot, The Origins, US, 1972
Fenton, Sasha	Fortune-Telling by Tarot Cards, Aquarian, UK, 1985
Fenton, Sasha	Tarot in Action, Aquarian, 1987
Frazer, Sir James	The Golden Bough, 1951
Gardner, Richard	The Tarot Speaks, UK, 1971
Gardner, Richard	Evolution through the Tarot, Weiser, US, 1977
Gerulski-Estes, Susan	The Book of the Tarot, Morgan & Morgan, US, 1981
Givry, Emile Grillot de	Witchcraft, Magic & Alchemy, France, 1929
Graves, Robert	The White Goddess
Gray, Eden	The Tarot Revealed, US, 1969
Hasbrouck, Muriel B	Tarot & Astrology, UK, 1941
Huson, Paul	The Devil's Picturebook, US, 1971
Kaplan, Stuart R.	Encyclopaedia of the Tarot 1 & 2, US Games, 1978
Knight, Gareth	The Treasure House of Images, Aquarian, 1985
Logan, Jo	Fortune-Telling by Tarot Cards, Blandford, UK, 1985
Mathers, S L Macgregor	The Tarot, Manuscript, UK, 1888
Montalban, Madeline	The Prediction Book of The Tarot, Blandford, UK, 1983
Newman, Kenneth D	The Tarot, Quadrant, US, 1983
Nichols, Sallie	Jung and Tarot, Weiser US, 1980
Papus	Tarot of the Bohemians, France, 1889
Peach, Emily	The Tarot Workbook, Aquarian Press, UK, 1984
Pollack, Rachel	The New Tarot, Aquarian Press, UK, 1989
Pollack, Rachel	78 degrees of Wisdom 1 & 2, Aquarian, UK, 1980
Pollack, Rachel	Tarot: The Open Labyrinth, Aquarian, UK, 1986
Sharman-Burke, Juliet	Complete Book of the Tarot, Pan, UK, 1985
Shephard, John	The Tarot Trumps, Aquarian, UK, 1985
Torrens, R G	The Golden Dawn, US, 1973
Wainwright, Liz	Articles in Arcana/FCTS, 1988
Waite, A E	Pictorial Key to the Tarot, UK, 1910
Wang, Robert	The Golden Dawn Tarot, Wesier, US, 1978

Picture Credits

The publishers would like to thank the following sources for their kind permission to reproduce the images as indicated in this book:

Corbis Bettmann 11; Mary Evans Picture Library 10,14,17top,18top; Ronald Grant Archive 9 ; Illustrations from the Papus Tarot Deck reproduced by permission of US Games Systems, Inc., Stamford, CT 06902 USA. Copyright ©1982 by US Games Systems, Inc. Further reproduction prohibited 16 top and bottom; Illustrations from the Papus Tarot Deck reproduced by permission of US Games Systems, Inc., Stamford, CT 06902 USA. Copyright ©1982 US Games Systems, Inc. Further reproduction prohibited 17 bottom; Ordo Templi 18 bottom left and right; Merlin Tarot Deck by Mr Stewart and Miranda Gray HarperCollins Publishers 20; Prediction Tarot Deck by Sasha Fenton HarperCollins Publishers 21.